POLICY PAPERS IN INTERNATIONAL AFFAIRS

*

NUMBER FIFTEEN

JAPANESE INDUSTRIAL POLICY

IRA C. MAGAZINER
& THOMAS M. HOUT

INSTITUTE OF INTERNATIONAL STUDIES
University of California
Berkeley

In sponsoring the Policy Papers in International Affairs series, the Institute of International Studies reasserts its commitment to a vigorous policy debate by providing a forum for innovative approaches to important policy issues. The views expressed in each paper are those of the author only, and publication in this series does not constitute endorsement by the Institute.

This work has been republished by the Regents of the University of California by kind permission and in agreement with the Policy Studies Institute, 1/2 Castle Lane, London, SW1E 6DR, by whom the work was first commissioned and published.

International Standard Book Number 0-87725-515-6

Library of Congress Card Number

Published 1981 by the Regents of the University of California

CONTENTS

LIST OF TABLES

LIST OF FIGURES

PREFACE TO THE AMERICAN EDITION

When this booklet was written—Summer 1978 to Summer 1979—the term *industrial policy* was not often heard in America. The activities of governments in Japan, France, Germany, and the United Kingdom to support industrial development and restructuring were little understood. They were generally viewed by policymakers in this country as dubious subsidies, or even unfair trade practices, with little redeeming economic value. We in the United States applied individual protectionist measures for our clothing, shoes, steel, televisions, ships, and some one hundred other products, but regarded these as unrelated pragmatic solutions to particular circumstances of international trade. Our Defense Department, National Aeronautic and Space Administration, and Energy Department provided huge grants to industry, but these were viewed as basic defense or energy policies.

We acknowledged as legitimate economic policy toward industry only macroeconomics and regulation. We allowed our currency to devalue to solve our trade deficit and blamed the lack of success on the Organization of Petroleum Exporting Countries (OPEC). Debate on the question of our ailing economy centered on Neo-Keynesianism, monetarism, deregulation, and supply side economics. Questions of industrial structure and competitive business economics were not actively discussed. Then, rude events in 1979 pushed the debate in new directions. OPEC redoubled the price of crude oil, our automobile industry was badly exposed, and Chrysler went to the edge. Automobiles became an overnight symbol of our competitive decline.

Official signs of American interest in the area first became evident as American officials began discussion of "reindustrialization." European and Japanese industrial policy officials in Europe and Japan began receiving American delegations whose "tune had changed" from accusations of unwise, unfair meddling by government in industrial affairs to questions about how to effectively conduct an industrial policy. Then in late Spring and Summer an encyclopedia's worth of articles began appearing on "reindustrialization" and "U.S. industrial decline." As often happens with ideas grown from crisis, they are initially seen as panacea, and then as it is realized that they are not, there is a strong reaction the other way. Ideas are elevated to great heights, torn down as dangerous, and rearranged into dozens of position papers—all before they are even well understood.

The U.S. debate on industrial policy as it now exists is reminiscent of how some European countries, particularly the United Kingdom, approached it for a decade. This debate is highly ideological and allows for a heady dose of posturing on the virtues of "the market system" by both sides while pointing to the incompetence of government and the greediness and shortsightedness of industry on opposing sides. The debate presents two polar options for industrial policy: (1) having the government select areas for investment by industry or (2) getting the government to reduce tax and regulatory constraints on investment. These poles are often characterized as "picking winners" versus "supply side economics," or "selective" versus "general" government role, or "government-initiated" versus "industry-initiated" solutions, etc. This jeopardizes the debate from the start.

This is not the place to go into discussions of American industry or industrial policy or to further assess this debate. However, if there are lessons from Japanese experience for the United States, they do not lie in copying specific patterns of organization or policy instruments used in Japan. Rather they lie in avoiding such ideological debates where industrial policy is concerned. Ideological debate of the sort we are beginning is the enemy of effective industrial policy. The key to successful industrial policy has to do with the discipline of analysis and consensus-forming mechanisms on specific issues rather than with broad policy principles.

As we note in our introduction, "industrial policy... cannot be properly studied or prescribed without a thorough understanding of how competition varies by industry and how the economics of businesses change over time.... Industrial policy is an integral part of the international competitive business system and must be highly responsive to it." The role of Japanese government in industry varies by the place of the industry in the international division of labor and by the competitive economic characteristics of the business. The discipline is that of business strategy. Government policy must be flexible enough and government policymakers knowledgeable enough to respond to individual conditions within industry.

Another major principle of this book is that the basis of success or failure in international trade rests with management at the business level. The government cannot be credited with Matsushita's success or blamed for Sasebo's failure. Government policy cannot be blamed for industry's ills in the United States either, or credited with its successes. The government can contribute to economic success or failure, but it is the management and workers in industry that are the important actors.

A final lesson is that the amount of money spent and size of bureaucracy do not correspond with effectiveness of policy. The Japanese government has relatively few officials concerned with industrial policy and has not spent huge sums. It is rather the competence of the individuals and the wise use of resources which are crucial.

All of this suggests that industrial policy is a delicate, subtle issue. There is more and less than meets the eye—particularly in Washington, where understanding of competitive industrial processes is thinly distributed, and in business circles, where the government is sometimes blindly viewed as the source of all evil. Industrial policy, as with macroeconomic policy, is in itself neither good nor bad. A great deal of careful analysis and thoughtful interaction must proceed, however, before useful policy mechanisms and directions begin to accumulate.

February 1981

ACKNOWLEDGMENTS

The authors share a common background with the Boston Consulting Group, where they have worked for clients on confidential assignments in a variety of industries and on a range of policy issues. These clients have included major Japanese companies as well as major Western companies and governments. The analysis of particular industries is excerpted primarily from this work. Similarly, the authors' acquaintance with Japanese industrial policy comes from client work, particularly that with Japanese corporations. Specific data references and sources accordingly must remain proprietary.

The authors gratefully acknowledge the research of Michiko Kato and the editorial assistance of Nancy G. Jackson and Susan Chira. Finally, they acknowledge a large debt to James C. Abegglen for his guidance and encouragement over many years.

I

INTRODUCTION

In order to understand Japan's success in international trade, it is necessary to have some appreciation of how Japanese companies compete internationally. It is interesting to see how many observers resort to special factors or uncommon mechanisms to explain Japan's success. These typically include a low priced and obedient labor force, producers' collusion at home, unfair trade practices, and government orchestration of the whole system. The implication is that these factors matter a great deal but are simply not available to other countries. These explanations are unsatisfactory less because they are untrue—for indeed some of these factors at some time played a part—but more because they miss the crucial points about the competitive process.

Japanese companies enjoy good growth and profitability by becoming low-cost producers. Where the Japanese succeed, they displace leading Western companies through a superior understanding of the competitive evolution of a business and a willingness to invest heavily for a sustained period of time. But they do not succeed in every industry. Japan has become the leader in steel but not in chemicals, in motorcycles but not in marine engines, and in consumer electronics but not in industrial electronics. In these less successful industries, the Japanese enjoy the same advantages of a well-disciplined labor force, a supportive government, easy access to debt financing, etc. Yet the Japanese remain marginal producers. This is no accident. It largely reflects the more astute strategies of the Western competitors.

The purpose of this study is to analyze Japan's industrial policy in the context of the basic competitive and economic forces which operate within all businesses. It is our view that industrial policy—which is defined here as the application of government resources and influence to industrial affairs—cannot be properly studied or prescribed without a thorough understanding of how competition varies by industry and how the economics of businesses change over time.[1] Industrial policy must be informed by more than national priorities and where the fast growth markets are. Industrial policy is an integral part of the international competitive business system and must be highly responsive to it. This is a major theme of this study.

Japan is a good subject because it illustrates this theme effectively. The Japanese have taken industrial policy seriously from their initial industrialization only a century ago. They have also developed a complex set of institutions and mechanisms across both the public and private sectors of the economy for hammering out and exercising industrial policy. It should be emphasized that most of these institutions and mechanisms have been fashioned by the nation's modern history; they represent accomplishments, not cultural inheritance.

If the first strength of Japanese industrial policy is competitive realism and economic logic, its second is the process which generates it. This policy by consensus approach is widely admired outside Japan and thinly understood. The Japanese, in the authors' experience, do not agree among themselves more readily nor subjugate one interest to another more easily than people in other countries. Policymaking there, as everywhere, is conflict resolution, and it is neither easy nor benign. The Japanese do, however, share a remarkably common view on the legitimacy of national government as guide and mediator. The bureaucracy is small and highly competent. The policy process, in both its formal and informal operation, is carefully geared to explore and resolve issues before a decision is made. Often, decisions are made acceptable to all participants or they are not made at all. Policy is often slow to emerge but usually is sound and widely implemented when it does.

Japanese industrial policy has been, in general, effective in the context we have defined, and our treatment of it here is essentially positive. We should, however, emphasize the limits of our aims. Our purpose is not a comprehensive statement of the origins and operation of Japan's industrial policy itself. That would take us deep into domestic politics and personalities in both government and business, well beyond our competence. Nor is it our intention to suggest Japan as a model approach to industrial policy analysis. The Japanese have made mistakes and experienced failures as the text will show. This study does not endorse Japan's approach.

[1] For a discussion of a competitive business economics and its relation to industrial policy, see Ira C. Magaziner et al., *A Framework for Swedish Industrial Policy* (Stockholm: Liberforelag, 1979).

Chapter II develops the context for industrial policy in Japan. It briefly describes the central long-term economic issues of the country and tracks the logic of its industrial policy historically. Then it focuses on particular Japanese industries and how they have succeeded or failed through the strategies of the major companies. Steel, motorcycles, and color television are briefly analyzed in these terms.

Chapter III deals with the question of who makes and influences industrial policy, what form it takes, and how the policy community interacts. This chapter describes not only the players in the process but analyzes in some detail the range of measures the government employs in executing policy.

Chapters IV to VI offer three pairs of case studies of policy in particular industries. These demonstrate how the course of policy is influenced differently by, and changes with, the stage of an industry's competitive cycle—early development and growth, healthy maturity, and eventual decline. In Japan, industrial policy is particularly active in the first and third stages, and inactive in the middle stage. The policy history of two currently healthy, internationally strong industries—steel and motor cars—is reviewed. The current attempts to ease the decline of the aluminum and shipbuilding sectors are described. Finally, the national effort to assist advanced industrial machinery and information electronics—two rapid growth industries where Japan is not yet competitively strong—is described. These case studies do not attempt to give full histories but rather seek to illustrate the themes of the earlier chapters.

II

JAPAN'S INDUSTRIAL POLICY: THE ECONOMIC BACKGROUND

The economics of Japan's industrial policy are straightforward. The objective is to help raise the real income of the population by assisting the shift of resources to the applications in which they can be most productive. The guiding force and discipline in this policy is that of international competitive advantage. Simply stated, this means that in an open economy a country's real industrial wage can rise sustainably over time only if its labor and capital flow toward increasingly higher value-added, higher productivity (per employee) businesses; the country's industry is then likely to become internationally cost-competitive in these businesses. The quality of Japanese industrial performance rests on the ability of both Japanese government and Japanese companies to operate successfully in this way. Broadly speaking, they have done so.

There are three main elements in Japanese industrial development:

(1) Recognition of the country's need to develop a highly competitive manufacturing sector;
(2) The deliberate restructuring of industry over time toward higher value-added, higher productivity industries (the Japanese call them "knowledge-intensive"); and
(3) Aggressive domestic and international business strategies.

These are three fairly simple and obvious ideas. Individually, they are unremarkable. Together, however, they explain very effectively the dynamic of Japanese performance.

JAPAN'S NEED TO EXPORT MANUFACTURED GOODS

Japan is essentially without natural resources, has little arable land, and did not industrialize until late in the nineteenth century. Accordingly, Japan's economic growth and development has been and continues to be dependent on imports of raw materials, energy sources, food, and technology. Japan is the world's largest importer of non-manufactured goods—roughly $60 billion in 1978—and of technology—roughly 25,000 separate licenses since the end of World War II. Japan cannot prosper without imports of these basic industrial inputs, and much of its modern political and military history grows from this single preoccupation.

Equally important, Japan needs to export to pay for the imports, and manufacturing has been and will continue to be the only means to obtain exports. Japan has little else to sell. It is not surprising, then, that the development and guidance of the producing sector—i.e., industrial policy—has been a central concern of its government and people since Japan came out of isolation and industrialized just over one hundred years ago.

This concern is carefully defined in the parliamentary authorization of the government's industrial bureaucracy to include all major elements in the producing system—raw materials sources, foreign exchange balances, technology, financial flows, quality of labor force and management, capital formation, and distribution (including ocean shipping). The need to export was a principal stimulus to policy, but the policy which has been developed addressed the more fundamental concern of the overall health of the producing system. Japan has no separate export policy in any meaningful sense of the term.

For all its trade success, Japan's exports of goods are a relatively low proportion of its gross national product. Table II.1 shows

Table II.1

EXPORTS OF GOODS AS PERCENT OF GROSS NATIONAL PRODUCT, 1960-1977

Country	1960	1970	1977
Belgium	33%	45%	47%
Netherlands	36	37	41
Switzerland	22	24	28
Sweden	18	21	26
United Kingdom	15	16	24
Germany	16	19	23
Japan	9	9	12
United States	4	4	6

Source: OECD Trade Statistics, Series A and B.

that Japan exported 12 percent of national output in 1977, well below most European economies. This reflects two important points. One, Japan has a large and a historically fast-growing domestic market—now the second largest non-Communist economy. Two, Japan is less well-integrated into its Asian regional economy than are the Western European nations. The Treaty of Rome is now twenty years old, while Japan took the first major steps to opening its market only ten years ago. Further specialization and increased regional trade can be expected in the future.

RESTRUCTURING OF JAPANESE INDUSTRY

Japan's government and business leaders have long shared the assumption that the composition of the country's output must continually shift if living standards are to rise. This shared attitude lies at the root of the industrial structure policy of the government and the very high investment rate of business. This belief was well-stated in a speech by Mr. Y. Ojimi, Vice Minister of International Trade and Industry, to the OECD Industrial Committee in Tokyo on June 24, 1970:

> Industrialization in developing countries will stimulate competitive relations in the markets of advanced nations in products with a low degree of processing. As a result, the confrontation between free trade and protectionism will become more intense.
>
> The solution of this problem is to be found according to economic logic, in progressively giving away industries to other countries much as a big brother gives his outgrown clothes to his younger brother. In this way, a country's own industries become more sophisticated.
>
> A solution of the North-South problem depends not only on internal development for developing nations but also on giving them fair opportunities in the area of trade. To do this, the advanced nations must plan for sophistication of their industrial structures and open their market for unsophisticated merchandise as well as offer aid in the form of funds and technology.

There is evidence of this restructuring in the composition of Japanese exports over time. Figure II.1 depicts this in the form of a diamond of changing contour. The diamond plots Japan's mix of total exports among four different categories of industry, each fundamentally different in its requirements for competitive success. Each point of the diamond locates Japan's position on one of the four coordinates (or industry categories). The bottom point of the diamond locates the percentage share of Japan's total exports in unskilled labor-intensive industries like clothing, light assembly, footwear, toys, etc. These industries require little capital investment or technology relative to the others. The right-hand point locates the share of capital-intensive industries which are machine- rather than process-oriented, such as motor cars, shipbuilding, light machinery, etc. These industries require high research and development expenditures, applications engineering, and marketing; many investments here are often regarded as part of current operating costs.

The shape of the diamond represents Japan's export mix in successive periods. In 1959 Japan's exports were mainly unskilled labor-intensive, and the diamond was skewed toward the bottom. Throughout the 1960s Japan's exports became more capital intensive—steel, motorcycles, ships, etc. By the mid-1970s, more complex products in the middle to upper areas of the diamond, such as motor cars and color televisions, became significant exports. This process is continuing as Japan's mix shifts toward high technology machinery and electronics industries. By 1985 the Japanese Economic Planning Agency hopes that Japan will have a structure similar to the structure of Germany's exports of manufactured goods in the mid-1970s (see dotted line in Figure II.1).

The evolution of Japan's industrial policy has led this shift in export mix. In the 1950s, labor-intensive products, such as textiles, were earning the foreign exchange for Japan. Policymakers recognized that increasing living standards required the development of capital-intensive industries rather than reliance on those where competitive advantage depended on low wage rates.

In the early 1950s, the government began funding the steel, chemical fertilizer, and shipbuilding industries. An explicit and more comprehensive industrial policy was developed in the late 1950s and 1960s. Scarce capital was directed to targeted industries, sometimes directly by government but more typically through the private banking system responding to the ministries' cues. A tax policy highly favorable to capital-intensive industries was developed, including protection for export earnings. Fragmented, undercapitalized industries, such as motor car parts and sewing machines, were consolidated at the government's initiative. Research and development in new industries like consumer electronics and downstream petrochemicals were publicly underwritten. Foreign investment into and out of Japan was sharply

Figure II.1 EVOLUTION OF JAPANESE INDUSTRIAL STRUCTURE

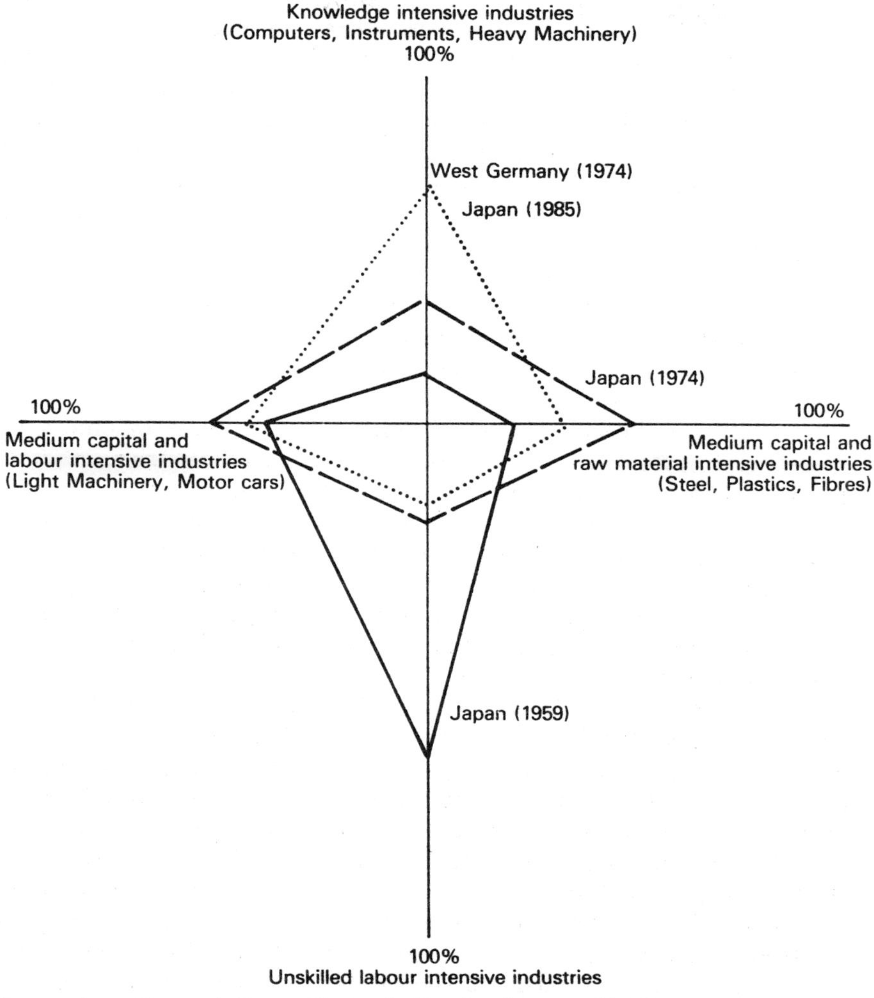

Source: *Japan Economic Survey,* Economic Planning Agency, 1974-75.

limited. Free trade was systematically rejected—manufactured imports were limited and exports were given a variety of incentives.

These policies and corresponding investments by industry had succeeded by the early 1970s. Japan had become the dominant supplier of steel, ships, motorcycles, and cameras to international markets. The trade balance swung into surplus, the yen became undervalued, foreign exchange accumulated, Japan was forced to open its borders to capital and products, and manufacturing wages and salaries rose annually by 10 percent in real terms.

In the early 1970s, Japan's industrial policy began to shift in recognition of Japan's new competitive position. The new policy as it has emerged has several threads. One has been to end assistance to the successful capital-intensive industries. Several like steel and motor cars are fully competitive and need no significant support. For heavy process industries like paper and pulp, aluminum, petrochemicals, and even steel, the policy has been to limit upstream[1] expansions to offshore sites only. This results from a desire to conserve energy, reduce pollution, spend foreign exchange, and, more fundamentally, to accelerate the shift in industrial structure. Other countries have better plant sites and lower cost energy—Japan can then export the plants and technology.

A second thread has been to assist the shift in Japan's industrial structure toward higher value-added, knowledge-intensive areas and to import more of the less sophisticated, labor-intensive manufactured goods. There were strong domestic reasons for this. Japanese producers were becoming uncompetitive in the latter area, and imports were needed to keep prices down in the overprotected domestic market. Moreover, Japan's industrial workplace had to learn to accommodate its people's rapidly increasing level of wages, skills, and aspirations.

Industrial policy, as a result, shifted its emphasis in the 1970s to knowledge-intensive[2] industries, where Japanese industry is, on average, still less advanced than its strongest Western competitors. (See Table II.2). Government support for research and development expenditure increased dramatically, and large joint government/industry development projects in computers and machine tools were started. Tax incentives for exports disappeared and were replaced by those for research and development, overseas investment, and pollution abatement. Japan Development Bank, the government's largest lender to the business sector, shifted new loans from large capital-intensive plants to computer leasing. Low-cost government export financing shifted from ships to entire plant exports, where financing is a key competitive variable.

[1]Upstream refers to early processing stages which usually are more capital- and energy-intensive than the finishing stages of production; the early processing stages are also potentially greater sources of pollution.

[2]See pp. 7-8 above.

Table II.2

JAPAN'S SHARE OF OECD EXPORTS, 1976: SELECTED EXAMPLES

Capital-intensive products	Percent
Motorcycles	90%
Televisions and radios	70
Ships	43
Steel	29
Watches	23
Motor cars	20
Knowledge-intensive products	
Electrical power machinery and switchgear	11
Heating and cooling equipment	10
Mechanical handling equipment	9
Metalworking machine tools	8
Construction equipment	8
Telecommunications equipment	7
Power tools	6
Specialty chemicals	5
Medical instruments	5
Aircraft	2

Source: OECD Trade Statistics, Series C.

A third thread of industrial policy in the 1970s has been the need to help manage the decline of competitively troubled industries. Textiles and chemical fertilizers were in trouble before the 1970s, but others like aluminum, shipbuilding, and synthetic textile fibers have become uncompetitive over the late1970s as the yen rose in value and newly industrializing countries moved into these businesses. The major tasks are to consolidate these industries by scrapping high cost capacity and encouraging small producers to merge. This has proved to be the most difficult of the 1970s policy directions.

Japan's industrial structure continues to change as international competitive forces operate, and the industrial policy has been a guiding factor. Over time, policy with respect to a particular industry has changed as its international competitive position has changed. On balance, Japan's industrial policy has been anticipating rather than reacting to international competitive evolution.

COMPETITIVE STRATEGIES OF JAPANESE COMPANIES

It takes more than rational industrial policy and evolution of industrial structure to establish international business leadership. Japan's export successes are the result of aggressive business strategies and competent management by Japanese companies in relation to their international competitors. Business competition is sustained conflict with an adversary. There are winners and losers. Although every competitive business confrontation has its own unique characteristics, a number of common principles determine success or failure.

The primary aim of any long-term competitive strategy is to achieve the lowest cost in producing and distributing a product. Industries differ in their production and market characteristics and in the competitors who are active; hence they require different strategies.

A common requirement for achieving a low cost position is the willingness to invest in physical capital. In most of Japan's successful industries, Japanese companies have invested more heavily and consistently than their Western competitors. Japanese companies typically evaluate investments differently from many Western companies. The latter usually isolate a project, grade it on a discounted cash flow rate of return basis, and closely observe its effect on the current earnings of the individual profit center.[3] This favors conservative, early return projects and penalizes more risky, long-term programs which may attempt a fundamental alteration of the business. The advantages of this method are its clarity and its bias against compounding mistakes in risky long-term programs. Also, in many Western companies, managers' salaries are often tied to the short-term performance goals of their individual profit center. In addition, managers are moved frequently from one branch to another. Projects which depress profitability even if they are expected to yield long-term competitive advantage may thus be discouraged.

Effective Japanese companies, on the other hand, typically view a business not as a series of discrete projects but as an integrated

[3]The profit center concept involves the assigning of individual profit goals and incentives to various subportions of a business. It is thought that this ensures more enthusiastic management at each level of the organization and provides clear mechanisms to evaluate management at all levels of an organization. In fact, in some cases it involves shortsightedness in strategic decision-making. Maximizing short-term profitability at the profit centers may conflict with the long-term profitability of the company as a whole.

business whose competitive position can be advanced or liquidated. Major investments are evaluated for their impact on competitive cost position and market share for the whole business over a several-year period. Japanese companies do not usually employ the profit center control system as often as Americans, and the compensation of management is less directly tied to this year's profit center performance. Accordingly, the Japanese typically find it easier to initiate investments in projects with a long-term payoff. Examples of such an investment might be a lower cost, higher volume plant which will require market share gains to fill capacity, or an extended research and development program which aims at radically redesigning a product. The hazards of this approach are that more capital is put at risk, and continuing commitments may be made to a business that is fundamentally not viable. However, in high-growth businesses where competition is still fluid and the outcome uncertain, the Japanese approach is usually superior.

Fixed capital investments are financed primarily by retained earnings and debt. By reputation, Japanese companies undertake large loans to finance their asset growth. This is an area, however, where generalizations can be misleading. In Japan's most successful industries, such as motorcycles, color television, motor cars, office copiers, forklift trucks, steel, shipbuilding, etc., companies did have a high debt/equity ratio in the growth years of the 1960s. Despite a closed home market, Japanese producers fought competitive battles with each other to build better products and bigger plants and to establish overseas distribution networks. The high Japanese market growth rates and intense competition helped the leaders who emerged to gain a strong position internationally.

In the 1970s, as cost advantage was secured against both marginal domestic competition and Western producers, loans were paid off and debt levels fell. With the exception of the capital-intensive steel and shipbuilding industries, successful Japanese companies in other industries have balance sheets and income statements which are comparable to their American and European counterparts. Their reward for investing more heavily than their competitors over the long growth period has been a low cost position and a more durable cash flow.

Where Japanese investments have succeeded, they have usually reduced the costs of manufacturing products and increased product reliability. This comes from achieving high volume output which, depending upon the business, allows for cost-effective product design and large-scale or long-run production. The Japanese success in motorcycles and television can be traced to the design of better components, the reduction in their number, and automated assembly.

In some businesses, the large-scale plant or machine is essential to a low cost position. Japan has the largest scale facilities in the world in a range of products from carbon steel to major electronic components (Tables II.3 and II.4). In other businesses, achieving high volume without proliferating the product mix is crucial to a low cost position; it enables long production runs and highly mechanized processes. Table II.5 illustrates sales volume per bearing design offered among major international bearings producers which, along with lower cost steel, explains Japan's strong cost position. A similar effect can be observed in motor cars and small diesel engines.

Table II.3

DEEPWATER WORLD-SCALE STEEL PLANTS, EARLY 1980s
(EXCLUDING USSR)

Plant	Country	Projected Capacity *(Million metric tons)*
Fukayama	Japan	16
Kashima	Japan	15
Kimitsu	Japan	14
Yawata	Japan	12
Oita	Japan	12
Chiba	Japan	10
Kagagawa	Japan	10
Mizushima	Japan	10
FOS	France	10
Taranto	Italy	10
Wakayama	Japan	9
Dunkirk	France	8
Nagoya	Japan	8
Hoogovens	Netherlands	6
Tabarao	Brazil	6
Pohang	Korea	6
Burns Harbor	United States	6

Source: Individual companies.

Table II.4

RELATIVE SCALE OF PRODUCTION FACILITIES FOR SELECTED COMPONENTS USED IN TELEVISION SETS, 1977

Components	Relative Production Scale	
	EEC	Far East
Cathode ray tubes	1	2.5
Line output transformers	1	2
Speakers	1	4
Integrated circuits	1	1
Diodes	1	1
Transistors	1	4
Fixed resistors	1	20
Potentiometers	1	10
Ceramic capacitors	1	10
Film capacitors	1	2
Aluminum capacitors	1	8
Tantalum capacitors	1	7

Source: Client study.

Table II.5

PRODUCTION OF BALL BEARINGS AMONG MAJOR INTERNATIONAL PRODUCERS

	Average for Major Japanese Producers	Timken (U.S.)	SKF (Sweden)	Fag (Germany)
Number of variants	10,000	12,500	25,000	25,000
Sales (billions[a] U.S. dollars)	1,417	820	1,492	671
Sales/variant	141.7	65.6	59.7	26.8

Source: Client assignment.

[a]Million million *not* thousand million.

The Japanese willingness to make investments which have a long payback period and their often superior production economics are related. Funds for product design and capital equipment, however, are only part of the necessary investment. Aggressive marketing and investment in distribution outlets are also required to enable full advantage to be taken of large-scale production.

Large-scale production usually requires a strong market share in a large home market plus aggressive exporting. Japanese companies historically have had the advantage of a large domestic market which was either closed or very expensive for foreign manufacturers to enter. Some Western firms persevered, and the Japanese market has been highly rewarding for them. Most, however, did not make the necessary investment in sales effort, and have suffered the competitive consequences. Their Japanese competitors took advantage of a large home market which enabled them to produce on a large scale and become cost competitive. The Japanese companies could then use the uncontested home market profits for aggressive market entry elsewhere in the world.

The market and product entry strategies of Japanese companies have often targeted the weak spots of competitors. Japanese companies commonly begin exporting to Third World markets which are peripheral to their large U.S. or European competitors. These markets represent a small portion of Western sales, but can add significantly to the Japanese company's volume base. When entering these markets, Japanese companies generally cut prices.

Often the Western company's manager in these markets is concerned about his current profitability and does not look beyond a two- or three-year period after which he can return to the home office. He is likely to sacrifice market share to a new, aggressive Japanese competitor rather than see a decline in current profits. As market share is often taken from market growth and thus does not affect current sales level, this is safer than sacrificing profitability. In this way, Japanese competitors replace Western companies in these small but growing markets and gain a stronger overall volume base with which to enter European or American markets.

Similarly, Japanese companies often enter a business at the simpler end of the product line, where the Western competitors often have lower profits. By aggressively pricing to gain market share, the Japanese company often causes its Western competitor to forfeit that part of the business. It was commonly thought that the Japanese might be hard to beat in the low end of the business, but would not be able to develop the products to threaten the main parts of the product range. In fact, as the motorcycle, television, camera, and motor car industries—plus a long list of industrial products—demonstrate, Japanese competition rarely stops with the "low end" of the business. The extensive experience, production volume, and distribution strength gained there can form a base for successful expansion.

When Japanese companies do enter the large markets and central parts of the product line which constitute the heart of a competitor's business, they tend to invest heavily in distribution, marketing, and "penetration pricing." Usually they expect to wait many years before the cash flow from these products and markets turns positive. As with cost-cutting capital investment, Japanese companies have shown a willingness to invest heavily in market penetration and to evaluate the investment with a long time horizon.

This brief tour of Japanese competitive behavior runs the risk of caricature. The patterns described do not hold for all Japanese companies nor do they exclude Western companies. A number of Western companies from computers to construction equipment and from specialty chemicals to apparel have approached international competition in similar fashion—a long investment time horizon, a preoccupation with market share and cost position, an aggressive market by market focus, etc. This behavior is by no means solely Japanese, but Japanese companies have provided some notable illustrations.

Steel. In 1950 the United States produced over 70 percent of total world steel, importing virtually none. It had the world's largest steel-producing facilities and thus, while it had the world's highest wage rates as well, was still the lowest cost producer. In 1958 the U.S. steel industry was estimated to be three times more productive per manhour than Japanese producers. Modernization of the Japanese steel industry proceeded rapidly during the 1950s, and output increased at 15 percent per year; nevertheless, Japanese companies remained high cost producers relative to the United States and exported less than 5 percent of their production.

During this period, the U.S. industry invested far less in physical capital than the Japanese and had a higher profit margin. Increases in productivity in the U.S. steel industry were less than one quarter of those of the Japanese industry. American companies were not as quick to take advantage of new technology offered by millmakers as were their Japanese counterparts.

By the early 1960s, Japanese total costs of production had reached U.S. levels, though their productivity did not match that of the U.S. steel industry until about 1970. Throughout the 1960s and early 1970s, although the rate of growth of domestic demand slowed down, the Japanese industry continued to expand production. This greater volume was absorbed by an increasingly aggressive export program and allowed Japanese steelmakers to build large, modern, efficient mills. Eleven new facilities constructed between 1952 and 1978 now account for over 80 percent of Japanese steel production (Table II.6). These mills are on average larger and more modern than their U.S. and European counterparts, and give the Japanese industry a cost advantage. In many steel processes, the cost per unit declines systematically with increasing volume. In blast furnaces, for example, this scale advantage amounts to a 30 percent reduction in production cost for every doubling in scale. In 1977 Japan had twenty-five blast furnaces capable of producing over two million annual tons

Table II.6

MAJOR JAPANESE STEEL PLANTS, 1965-1973

Company	Name of Plant	Year of First Operation	1973 Output (Million metric tons)	Projected Capacity (Million metric tons)
Nippon	Kimitsu	1965	9.0	14.0
	Yawata	1959	9.8	12.0
	Sakai	1961	4.4	4.3
	Nagoya	1958	6.2	7.3
	Oita	1971	3.5	12.0
NKK	Fukayama	1965	11.8	16.0
Kawasaki	Chiba	1952	6.1	6.5
	Mizushima	1961	7.9	10.0
Sumitomo	Wakayama	1960	7.2	9.5
	Kashima	1967	5.2	15.0
Kobe	Kogogawa	1968	4.4	10.0
TOTAL			75.5	116.6

Source: Clients assignment.

in volume; the United States had none, and the European Economic Community only seven (Table II.7).

Table II.7

WORLD'S LARGEST BLAST FURNACES IN 1977

Location	Number of Furnaces Over Two-million-tons Capacity	
	In Operation	Under Construction
Japan	25	9
USSR	9	5
EEC	7	6
United States	0	3
Other:	0	5
Poland		1
Brazil		3
Austria		1

Source: Client study.

Most expansion in the United States during this period occurred in roundout[4] fashion in order to minimize investment and risk and to maintain current profitability and dividends. Only one greenfield[5] facility was constructed. Roundout investment tends to be highly inefficient, since a new strip mill or finishing mill is placed wherever there is space on the existing steel plant site. Materials handling, rework, and internal transport costs become far greater than in a greenfield plant, which can be designed in line with the natural flow of the product. The more efficient product flow of the new Japanese plants represents a further advantage over American producers.

The Japanese industry also invested to overcome inherent disadvantages in raw materials. By building ships that could carry large quantities of iron ore and coking coal, they were able to transport high quality ore and coal from Australia and Brazil to Japan at costs comparable to those required to bring lower quality ore from Minnesota to Ohio or Pennsylvania (Table II.8). Japanese companies also

[4]A roundout investment is one in which a new piece of equipment is placed at an already existing mill.

[5]A greenfield facility is one which is built completely from the ground up on a new site.

Table II.8

AVERAGE TRANSPORT COSTS OF IRON ORE

Area/Year	Constant (1973) Dollars per Ton
All Japanese mills and mines	
1964	$8.00
1965	7.12
1966	6.20
1967	5.36
1968	4.87
1969	4.45
1970	4.52
1971	3.93
1972	3.45
1973	3.50
Upper Minnesota to Chicago (Great Lakes)	
1973	3.50
Upper Minnesota to Pittsburgh	
1973	6.50

Source: Client study.

made heavy financial investments in these overseas mines in order to guarantee their sources of supply. Ultimately, the proximity of U.S. mills to domestic sources of coal or iron ore became a drawback rather than an advantage. Japanese mills constructed at sites with access to deepwater ports were better able to take advantage of newly developed, higher quality, lower cost sources of raw materials.

Thus Japan built the world's most efficient steel industry. The venture required both massive capital investment and aggressive pursuit of export markets to support continued rapid growth despite decreases in the rate of growth of home consumption. In the crucial years when Japan gained its productivity advantage over the United States, the Japanese steel industry increased its physical capital by over 23 percent a year compared to only 4 percent for the United States, despite a lower average rate of return on capital (1.8 percent for the Japanese big five companies and 3.8 percent for the largest eight U.S. companies). The Japanese incurred a marginal debt-to-equity ratio of almost 11 to 1[6] during these years, allowing a satisfactory return on equity and guaranteeing the continued improvement of their competitive productivity (Table II.9).

[6]All short- and long-term debt is included.

Table II.9

FINANCING OF JAPANESE STEEL INVESTMENT, 1966-1972

Major Japanese steel companies	Percent/Ratio
Asset growth per year	23.6%
Average return on assets 1966-72	1.8%
Average return on equity 1966-72	20.0%
Marginal debt to equity ratio, 1966-72	11:6.1
Debt to equity ratio, 1972	6:3.1
Cash sources for financing	**Percent**
Debt	91.1%
Retained earnings	1.1
New Equity	7.9

Source: Annual reports and balance sheets of the major steel companies.

The U.S. steel industry's underlying assumptions about the business prevented it from making the aggressive investments in modernization that would have been needed to match the pace of Japanese investment. From the U.S. company's point of view, the discounted cash flow return from a new low-cost greenfield steel mill could not justify its construction. Levels of debt as high as the Japanese industry's were unthinkable, and since no attempts were made to export in large quantities, growth rates were too slow to justify the large additions to capacity. The limited modernization investments which the companies made did not protect the U.S. industry's leadership in world markets.

The increase in exports of the Japanese steel industry did not come easily. Japanese companies made large investments in more than fifty finishing facilities in developing countries in order to establish a base for steel exports. Penetrating the wary U.S. and European markets, moreover, required large initial marketing investments. The Japanese industry was prepared to make these investments and to await a long-term payback.

Although the success of the Japanese steel industry thus reflects a combination of valid assumptions, appropriate attitudes, and intelligent decisions, it is also due in part to the sluggishness of its competition. In industries where U.S. and European producers have responded more alertly, the Japanese approach has been less successful.

In most commodity industries, costs (and prices) decline in real (inflation-adjusted) terms as production experience is gained.[7] Twenty to thirty percent cost reductions with each doubling of accumulated production are fairly characteristic of most industries. Prices usually follow costs down a similar curve in the long term. In the U.S. steel industry, however, prices actually increased in real terms during the late 1940s and 1950s. When the first Japanese imports entered the market in 1959, prices began to decline; in 1968, when the first voluntary restraint agreements on Japanese imports to the United States were instituted, prices again began to climb (Figure II.2).

Figure II.2

EXPERIENCE CURVE—U.S. STEEL INDUSTRY, 1946-1974

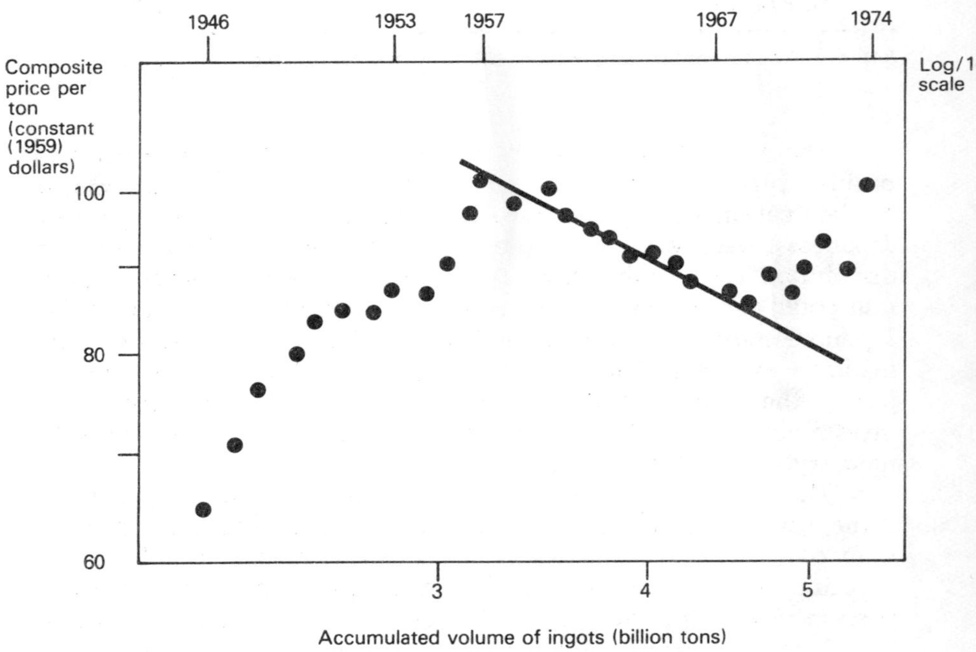

Source: Client study.

[7]This effect is known as the "experience curve." For a detailed account of "experience curves," see *Perspectives on Experience* (Boston Consulting Group, 1971).

In the high-growth stainless steel sheet sector, the U.S. industry prices remained constant in the late 1940s and 1950s, while the Japanese prices declined along an "experience curve" with a slope of 70 percent—i.e., prices dropped 30 percent with each doubling of cumulative production (Figure II.3). Japanese prices fell below those of the United States in the late 1950s. (Had the U.S. industry achieved even modest decrease in costs and prices during this period, it could have preempted Japanese growth and ability to export.)

A look at other industries suggests that aggressive efforts to cut costs did protect the original leading position. In polyethylene plastic resin, for instance, the U.S. industry prices declined along a 25 percent slope between 1950 and 1969 (Figure II.4). While a number of the strongest companies in Japan have entered this business, the Japanese industry generally lags behind strong U.S. and European competitors in size of plant, technology, productivity, and export success. In low density polyethylene, Japanese producers operate on a smaller scale than their American and European counterparts, and in high density polyethylene, where technology plays a big role, American and European competitors have kept a process technology lead over Japanese producers with the exception of Mitsui.

Figure II.3

COMPARATIVE EXPERIENCE CURVE—STAINLESS STEEL SHEET

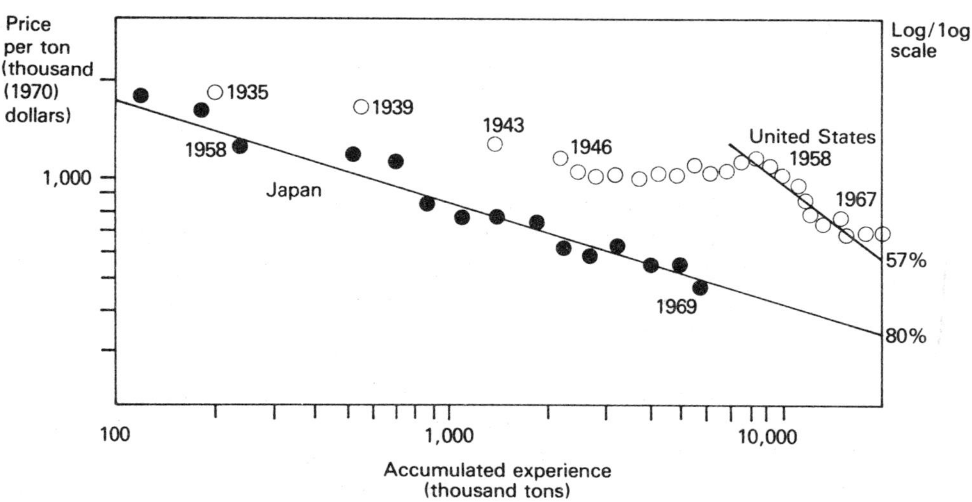

Source: Client study.

Figure II.4

EXPERIENCE CURVE—U.S. LOW DENSITY POLYETHYLENE FILM INDUSTRY, 1959-1969

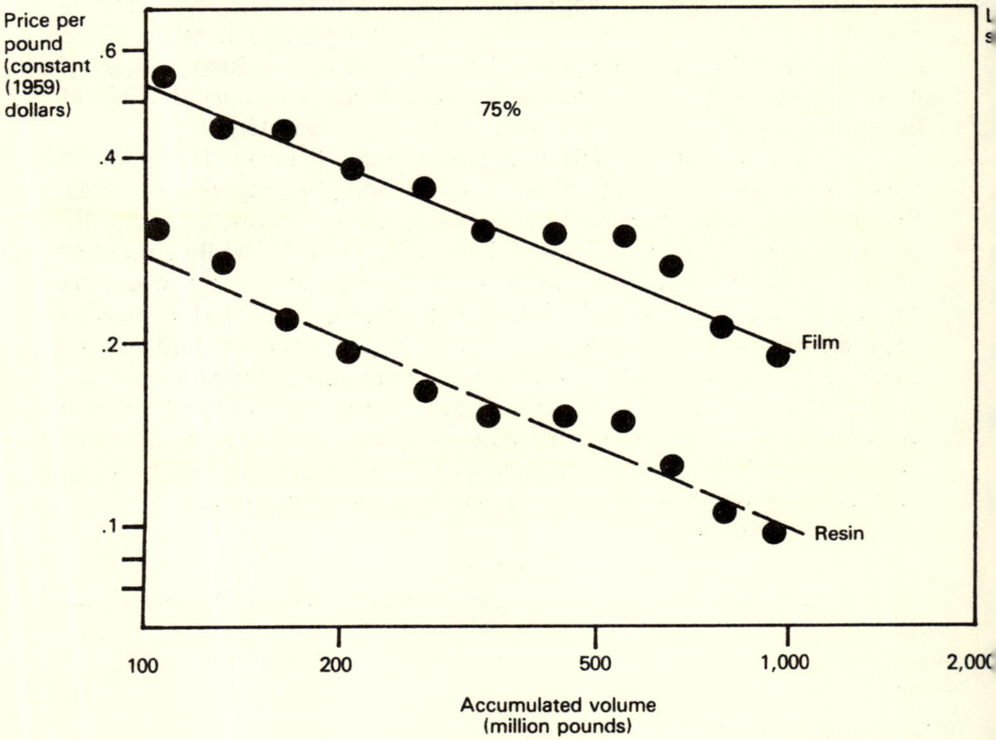

Source: Client study.

To reduce the difference between Japan's success in steel and its record in polyethylene industries to a single factor would be an oversimplification. But there is little question that the sluggishness of the strategies of Western competitors in some industries has largely determined the success of Japan's postwar industrial growth.

Motorcycles. The large-size motorcycle industry provides another illustration of Japanese competitive success. The United States is easily the largest motorcycle market in the world, and leadership there is crucial in securing the top international position among producers. There is only one domestic producer in the United States—Harley-Davidson. In 1968 the United Kingdom manufacturers, who have traditionally been world volume and style leaders in motorcycles over 450 cc in engine displacement, held 49 percent of the U.S. market (in units), and seven of the fifteen models sold were British. Japanese producers—including Honda, Yamaha, Kawasaki, and Suzuki, who were very active in the small-size motorcycle market—sold only 22 percent of the large-size units.

Between 1968 and 1974, the U.S. market for motorcycles grew at 25 percent a year; part of this growth was due to cyclists replacing smaller units with larger bikes. By 1974 Japanese producers had 77 percent of the market while the U.K. share had fallen to roughly 10 percent. The number of Japanese models rose from three to thirteen while the number of British models actually declined.

Japanese success in this industry again reflects a flagging effort on the part of its competitors. Investment in the U.K. industry was low; production levels had not grown, production methods remained unchanged, productivity was stagnant, innovation lagged, and the distribution network was not maintained. The Japanese, on the other hand, had established leadership in the smaller size market during the 1960s and extended their product line upward as the market shifted.

Competition among the four Japanese producers was central to the overall Japanese success. Selling more in the large U.S. market was critical to remaining competitive in production efficiency at home, and it is not surprising that by the middle 1970s exports were over one half of total Japanese production (from 4 percent in 1960). The Japanese producers competed for U.S. dealerships and customers through new product introduction, better warehousing and spare parts services, image building campaigns, and price competition. Honda, the leader, was aggressively pursued, particularly by Yamaha. Each of the four gained a share of the U.S. market over the period through quite independent business strategies.

This growth was accomplished without inherent advantages in wage rates or government assistance. Indeed by 1970 wage rates in this industry were higher in Japan than in the United Kingdom. Japanese productivity levels, however, were dramatically higher as a result of highly specialized, large-scale production facilities. The Japanese factories are far larger than their British counterparts (Table II.10). Once again, the high investment, high volume approach of the Japanese manufacturers allowed them to overtake their more sluggish Western competitors.

Color Television. The Japanese consumer electronics industry grew up in the late 1950s and early 1960s around unskilled labor-

Table II.10

COMPARATIVE MOTORCYCLE PRODUCTION AND PRODUCTIVITY, 1975

Producer	Motorcycle Output (000 units)	Motorcycles per Man Year[a]
Honda (Japan):		
Suzuki	1,500	350
Hamamatsu	500	174
Kawasaki (Japan)		
Akashi	300	159
Norton-Villiers-Triumph (U.K.):		
Meriden	28	14
Wolverhampton	18	18
Harley-Davidson (U.S.)	38	11
BMW (Germany)	25	20

Source: Client study.

[a]Includes Japanese subcontracts.

intensive component insertion. Using processes licensed from U.S. and European companies, Japanese manufacturers based an overall competitive cost advantage on their relatively low wage rates. During the late 1960s, a strong group of independent Japanese companies emerged, although the Japanese industry was not yet a significant factor in world exports. Many felt that the rapid increase in wage rates and the appreciation of the yen that began in the early 1970s would spell the demise of the industry.

In 1970, productivity in television set manufacture was slightly lower in Japan than in Europe and the United States, and Japanese capability in set design lagged behind that of their world competitors. Production volumes were relatively low and the industry exported only a small proportion of its output (17 percent). By 1978 Japanese productivity in set assembly was three to five times greater than that of its major world competitors (Figure II.5), and Japanese producers controlled over half of non-Comecon color television sales (Table II.11). These advances occurred despite rapid increases in Japanese wage rates and the appreciation of the yen (Figure II.6).

Japanese success in this industry is due once again to rapid growth and investment—in this case directed toward process engineering and

Figure II.5

AVERAGE NUMBER OF HOURS REQUIRED TO ASSEMBLE 20-INCH COLOR TELEVISION SET, 1977

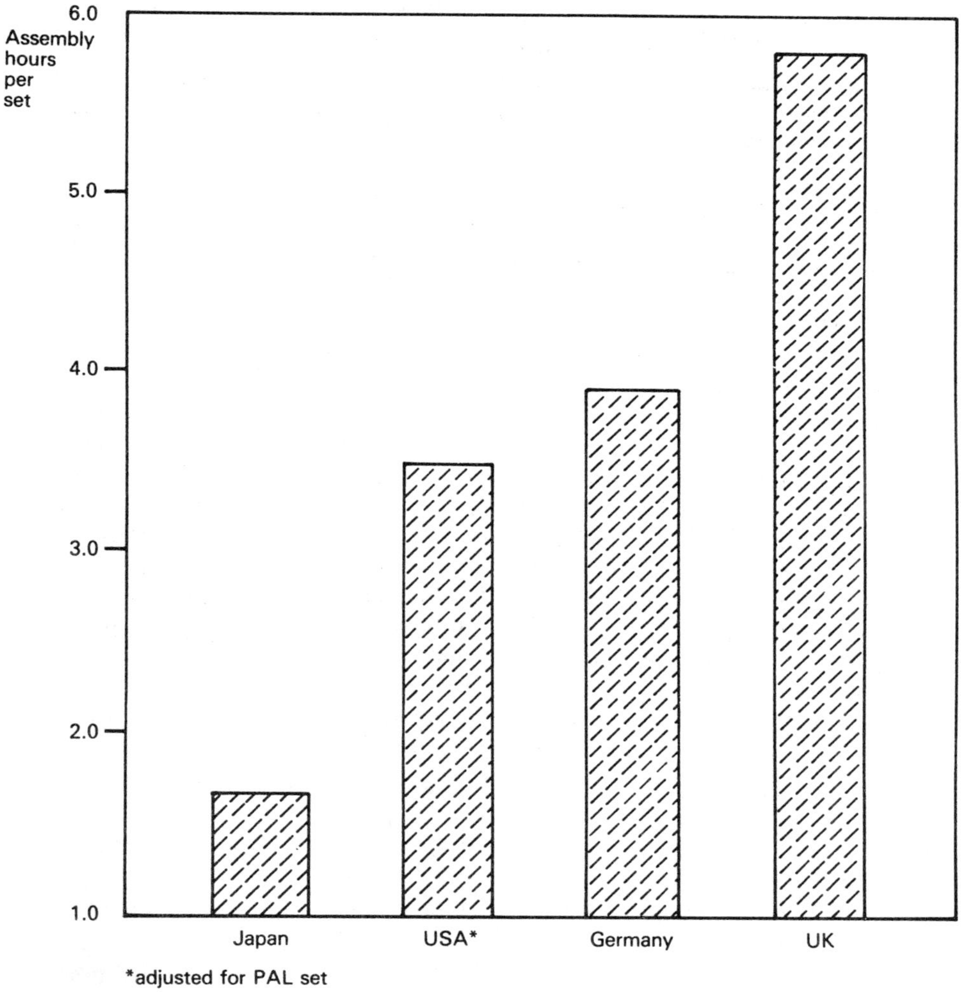

Source: Client assignment.

product engineering to obtain lower production costs and to improve set reliability. Since 1972 the Japanese producers have lowered the time required to assemble a color television from approximately six

Table II.11

JAPANESE COLOR TELEVISION INDUSTRY, 1977

Market	Market Size	Japanese Products Made in Japan	Japanese Local Production	Controlled by Japan	Share
	(Millions of units)				Percent
Japan	5.3	5.3	—	5.3	100%
United States	9.1	2.1	1.4	3.5	39
Europe	9.0	.6	.3	.9	10
Other countries	5.4	1.6	1.0	2.6	48
TOTAL	28.8	9.6	2.7	12.3	43

Source: Client study.

man-hours to about one-and-a-half man-hours. Three factors determined this increase in productivity: a reduced number of components in a set, an increased use of automation in insertion and materials handling, and a reduced number of circuit boards in a set.

Fewer components means less assembly time and a lower materials cost in a set. While the average PAL[8] system television set made in Europe had about 600-650 components in 1978, the comparable Japanese set had less than 500. This results primarily from the use of integrated circuits with a higher level of integration than those used by European setmakers, and the use of preconverged picture tubes.

In 1978 roughly 70 to 80 percent of all electrical components in a Japanese television set were automatically inserted. European producers average somewhere between 15 and 30 percent. In addition, Japanese sets are designed to minimize insertion times by the machines and to allow a high degree of automation in testing during the insertion process. Many Japanese factories have also achieved high degrees of automation in inventory control and final set assembly, including the use of robots in certain functions.

Japanese sets have also achieved significantly higher reliability both in the factory and in the field than Western-produced sets

[8]PAL=Phase Alternating Line.

Figure II.6

COMPARATIVE TOTAL EMPLOYMENT COSTS PER HOUR—TELEVISION SET ASSEMBLY (MOVING EXCHANGE RATE BASIS), 1968-1978

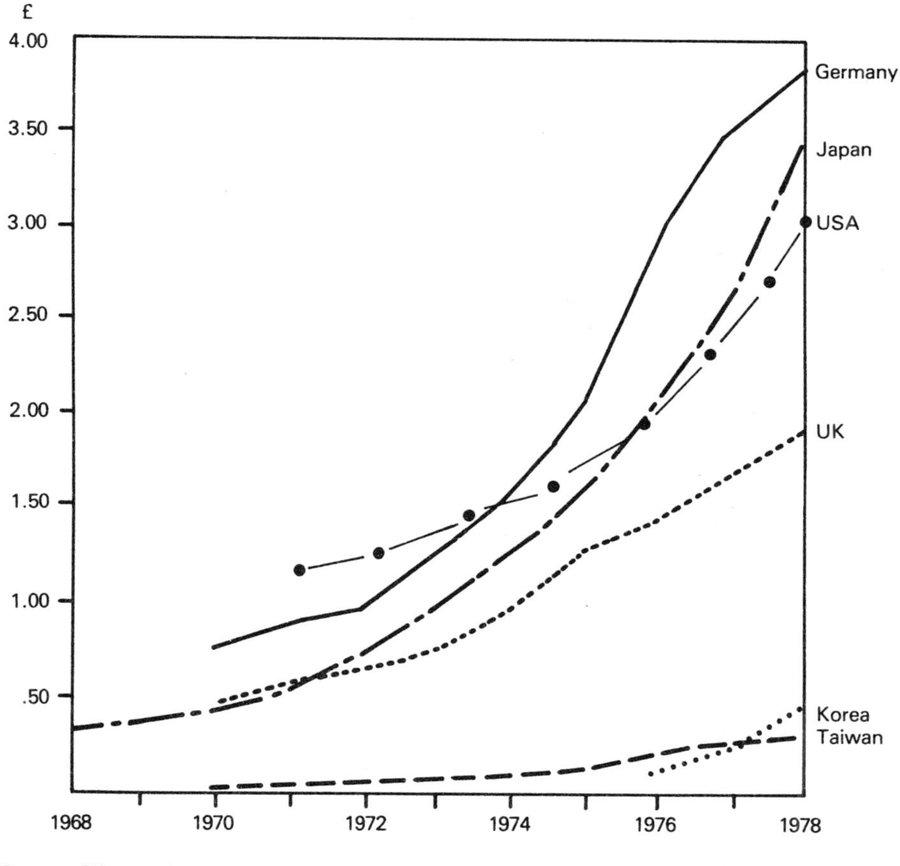

Source: Client assignment.

(Figure II.7). This superiority results from a higher degree of preproduction component testing, greater component testing of insertion, and longer production runs of each chassis design, allowing superior design "debugging."

All of these improvements depend to some extent on scale. Preproduction testing is feasible when producing over half a million sets a year, as do Japanese factories, but more difficult when producing only one hundred thousand, as in the United Kingdom.

Figure II.7

COLOR TELEVISION SETS—FIELD CALL RATE AND PRODUCTION FALL-OFF

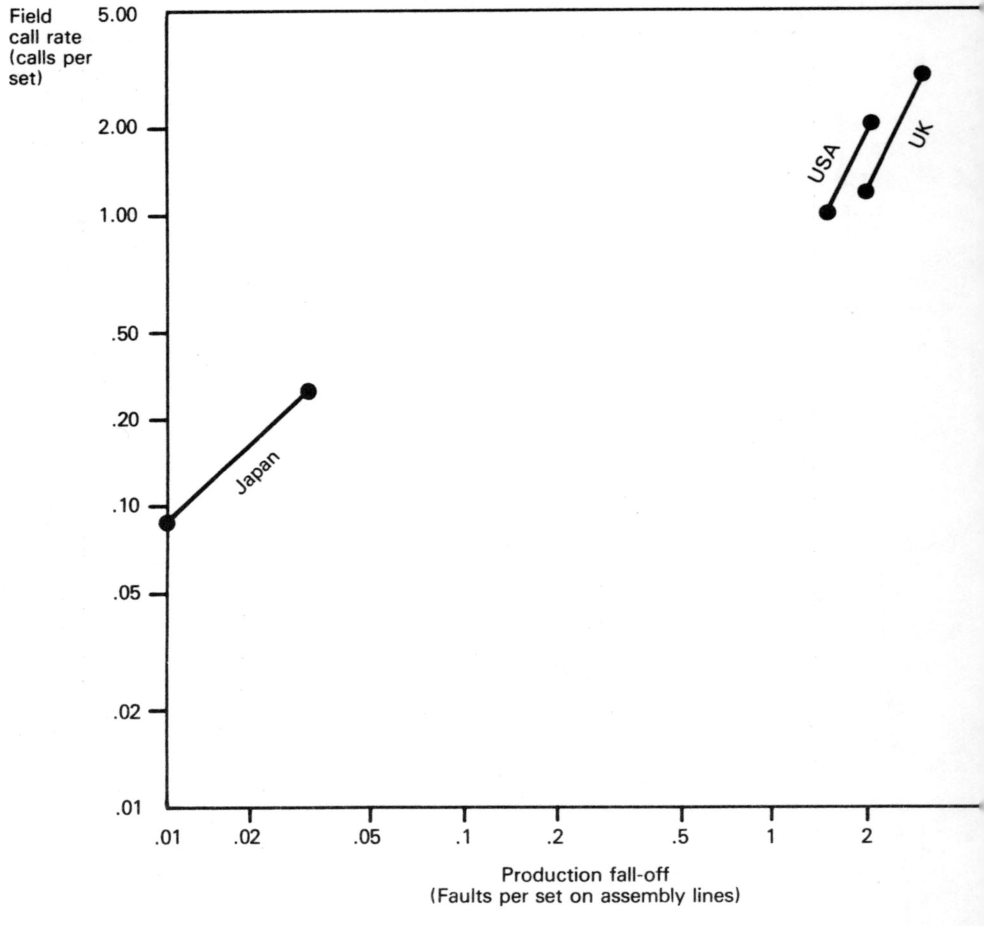

Note: The dots in the diagram represent the range for surveyed sets.
Source: Client study.

Japanese producers have surpassed their Western competitors both in average factory volume (700,000 in Japan, 150,000 in the United Kingdom, for example) and in cumulative volume per chassis type (1.2 million in Japan, 400,000 in Europe). The Japanese strategy of investing heavily and marketing aggressively to gain market share has encouraged ever-increasing efficiency. In addition, it has enabled Japan to minimize employment dislocations, as jobs lost through automation are partially offset by jobs created by growth.

Japanese and Western producers have also responded differently to rising labor costs. While Japanese manufacturers concentrated on product and process engineering to reduce the labor content of the set, many U.S. and European competitors have opted to move production offshore to countries with low wage rates. As late as the early 1970s, if companies in Europe and the United States had pursued more aggressive export strategies together with process and product engineering, they could have maintained a leadership position vis-à-vis Japanese producers. They did not choose that course.

As in steel and motorcycles, Japanese success in color television has been due both to strategic initiatives—aggressive investment for cost reduction and an increase in exports when home growth was slowing down—and to the weak response of competitors.

SOME WESTERN SUCCESSES

Japanese industry does not always achieve success in overtaking Western companies. As mentioned earlier, in polyethylene and many parts of the chemical industry, Western companies have successfully fought off challenges from major Japanese companies. In other industries, such as aluminum and forest products, Japan's raw materials disadvantages have prevented it from developing competitive industries.

More significant, however, are a number of industries where aggressive Japanese companies attempted but failed to overtake Western leaders with strategies similar to those used in the consumer electronics or car industries. In these cases—in industries as diverse as construction equipment, plate heat exchangers, chain saws, and marine engines—aggressive U.S. and European business strategies have frustrated Japanese efforts.

European and U.S. companies in these businesses moved into the Japanese market early, sustaining the losses and high investment necessary to build secure market positions. This strategy prevented the Japanese from taking full advantage of their home market base. The operations in Japan of IBM, Caterpillar, Eastman Kodak, Omark, and others are examples. In addition, the astute competitor has blunted early the Japanese thrust into third markets, either preventing gains in the Japanese share of the market or at least making any gains extremely costly.

Competing against a competent Japanese company requires extraordinary perspective and determination. In the future, we are likely to see some high-powered competition between strong Western leaders and aggressive Japanese challengers in a number of knowledge-intensive businesses. Many Western companies in these industries have learned from the past and will not display the weaknesses characteristic of Western companies in steel, televisions, and motorcycles.

MYTHS ABOUT JAPANESE COMPETITION

After this review of Japan's record in three major international industries, we are in a position to reconsider some frequent claims about Japanese competitive behavior.

Japan's low wage rates during the 1960s and early 1970s are often cited as a reason for Japan's success. Wages were lower than major Western competitors, and for this reason Japan was able to compete even when its product design, production technology, and plant scale—i.e., factors that determine productivity—were inferior. As Japanese productivity achieved parity in a number of industries by the early and mid-1970s, the value of the yen was slow to respond, and the Japanese cost advantage increased. This situation tended to correct itself as Japan's wages and salaries rose rapidly relative to those in Western countries and as the value of the yen eventually rose as well.

Even though low wages did provide some initial advantage, this was not an essential cause of industrial success. Had Japanese wages been significantly higher in the 1960s and early 1970s, gains in the share of the international market by Japan would have occurred, but might have taken longer. The rate of Japanese productivity increase would have been the same or even higher. Japanese capital investment was largely intended to reduce labor costs and to increase reliability. A higher wage rate would have provided greater incentive to invest so that labor would be used more efficiently. The fact is that Western competitors underestimated the Japanese ability to continue to increase productivity. They believed that rising Japanese wages would solve their competitive problems. It is interesting to speculate whether a higher wage rate (more respectable in Western eyes) would have caused competitors to take the Japanese more seriously.

Another claim sometimes made about Japanese competitive behavior is that the Japanese used export markets to achieve their initial growth. This is not the case. In steel, motor cars and motorcycles, and television sets, exports took a relatively small share of total output until the home market was large and saturated (Table II.12). Only then did the export ratio begin to increase significantly. Strong export positions were built only when domestic markets were approaching saturation.

Table II.12

EXPORTS AS PERCENT OF OUTPUT IN JAPAN, 1966-1976: SELECTED PRODUCTS

Year	Color Television	Motor Cars	Steel	Motorcycles
1966	14%	14%	27%	40%
1968	18	15	26	46
1970	17	23	25	60
1972	22	35	30	70
1974	33	43	37	75
1976	51	49	44	72

Source: Ministry of International Trade and Industry (Japan).

Another claim is that Japanese competitors often sell products into foreign markets at unfairly low prices. In a number of cases, charges of Japanese dumping have been upheld by U.S. and European government investigation. But the volume of total Japanese exports covered by these findings is modest. It is often entirely reasonable for any competitor seeking to penetrate a well-developed market to price very aggressively and, if necessary, challenge the anti-dumping statute. The Japanese in a number of industries have done this.

The problem is that most dumping allegations are simply wrong or badly timed. Dumping is a highly technical finding, requiring many adjustments to be made to export and domestic prices before comparing them. Most investigations disappoint the party bringing the charge, for what appeared to be unfairly low pricing turns out to be based on a competitor's superior cost position. Even the charges with merit usually are made too late to matter. When the Japanese dump, they will usually do it when newly entering a market—

before their product is known and acceptable on attributes other than price. Once established, the product typically commands a higher and higher price. In fact, in a large number of highly accepted Japanese products such as steel, motorcycles, color television, and motor cars, Japanese export prices to the United States during lengthy periods in the middle and late 1970s have been significantly higher than prices to the Japanese domestic market.

A final issue is the "Japan Inc." allegation, whereby government and business collude to further Japan's exports, often at the expense of the domestic consumer. The view asserts a commanding industrial role for government. The next chapter discusses the industrial role of government at length.

III

JAPANESE INDUSTRIAL POLICY: THE IMPLEMENTATION PROCESS

The previous chapter discussed production and distribution possibilities (valid for most industrialized countries) underlying Japanese industrial policy. More distinctly Japanese is the process by which industrial policy is determined and carried through. In this chapter we consider some key aspects of the industrial policy process in Japan. We begin with attitudes which create a favorable climate for successful industrial policy. We then explore the roots of industrial policy in Japanese history and describe the major institutions involved in policy formulation and implementation. Finally, we describe policy objectives and instruments and try to counter some false impressions often voiced in the West about how Japanese industrial policy operates.

THE UNDERLYING ATTITUDES

Many business leaders in the United States and in Europe view any government initiatives toward industrial policy with suspicion and hostility. Not surprisingly, many conservative political leaders identified with the business community in these countries tend to oppose national industrial policy on ideological grounds. On the other side, progressive political parties tend to distrust big business and the motives of its leaders. Historically, the state assumed an active economic role in Western economies in order to correct what were considered to be the private sector's economic and social failures.

Japanese historical tradition, on the other hand, grants to government a legitimate role in shaping and helping to carry out industrial policy. Japanese businessmen share with government leaders and officials a sense of the importance of coordinated national development, and are generally amenable to and in fact expect government intervention to advance this goal. Senior businessmen view government guidance of industry as a normal state of affairs. They may not always enjoy the process or approve the specific actions, but they see the process as legitimate and in the main useful. While business leaders are of course primarily concerned with the success of their individual firms, many actually identify the success of their companies with the greater good of Japan. This is somewhat less true of the younger generation of management, but it remains a very strong thread of the Japanese mentality.

In Japan there is a strong tradition of bureaucrats overseeing industrial affairs. The Diet's acts enunciate only essential policy, and give broad charter to the ministries. The ministries are staffed by a competent core of career officials, many of whom enter politics when they retire from the ministry. This pattern has provided good working relations between the Diet and the ministries.

Diet members do have considerable influence, particularly in the appointment of staff to ministries and in tax and expenditure policies. To the ministries, however, belongs the responsibility for developing coherent programs, drafting legislation, and carrying it out with broad discretion. Changes in the Diet's composition and mood do not greatly move the boundaries of the ministries' authority and effectiveness in industrial policy matters.

HISTORICAL ROOTS OF INDUSTRIAL POLICY

Although the substance of Japan's industrial policy has changed significantly during the postwar period, the process has remained relatively stable, retaining characteristics of the policy that accompanied Japan into the modern world with the Meiji Restoration a century ago.

In 1868 Japan was abruptly opened to world trade after centuries of economic isolation. The density of the population and the mountainous landscape ruled out large-scale agriculture and dictated industrialization as the path to higher income and trade. The government's response to this challenge set the tone for Japanese industrial policy to follow. Japan's new leaders recruited an elite, central bureaucracy from the able clan samurai whose interests were nationalist and whose perspective was modern. Isolated from the Western debate on political economy (socialism versus capitalism), they were pragmatic rather than ideological in their thinking. They did not fear concentration of industrial or financial power, and in fact encouraged such concentration as a point of contact and coordination with the central ministries. Rapid capital accumulation had to be encouraged.

After some limited early experiments in state entrepreneurship, the government played only a small direct or regulatory role in the nineteenth-century's rapid industrialization of Japan, but the state, as an architect, catalyst, and coordinator of industrial policy, dominated the policymaking process.[1]

Westerners puzzled by the centripetal nature of this process should bear in mind that the origins and rationale of the state's authority are remarkably different from those of our own tradition. Japanese statism is rooted in familism.

> In the traditional view, the whole nation is a family; what the house is to a biological family, the state is to the national family. The state is not merely a part of the system, but the very framework of it. The Japanese feel that in the beginning there was the nation house called Japan and the people were born into it. . . . The state bureaucrats exercise authority not in the name of the people, but in the name of the House of Japan. To the Japanese way of thinking, then, the state does not "interfere" with the affairs of private business. It merely manages itself, exercising authority and control of its constituencies. The productive activities of private businesses is very much a part of the business of the whole nation-state.[2]

Of course, familism does not fully describe the relations between the private sector and the government in Japan. Conflicts of interest do exist between the business community and the state as in the West, but there is a clear sense of common purpose—born probably of Japan's long isolation—and, more importantly, a commonly accepted and extremely well-developed process to resolve conflict.

POLICYMAKING INSTITUTIONS

To understand the ways in which this interaction occurs, it is necessary to know something of the various agencies and groups involved. In addition to government agencies, a wide variety of public institutions, such as publicly funded banks, play a key role in industrial policy, as well as a wide variety of private institutions, such as

[1]For further discussion, see William W. Lockwood, *The Economic Development of Japan* (Princeton: Princeton University Press, 1954).

[2]K. Haitani, *The Japanese Economic System* (Lexington, Mass.: Lexington Books, 1976).

business management associations, trade associations, and the city banks. These private institutions serve as intermediaries between the ministries and companies, and typically assist in research into policy initiatives and also help to implement policies. The intricate web of interaction among the ministries, the public companies, the private associations, and the city banks forms the core of what is normally called the informal consensus building in Japanese industrial policy. Though complex and informal, these processes do form regular patterns.

KEY GOVERNMENT AGENCIES. Two agencies of government—the Ministry of Finance (MOF) and the Ministry of International Trade and Industry (MITI)—deserve extended discussion. The Economic Planning Agency, while it puts together indicative long-term economic plans and studies the economy's interdependencies, plays a lesser role in industrial policymaking.

Ministry of Finance. The MOF sets monetary and fiscal policies and controls the government's budgeting and tax-collection operations. Because the principal instruments of industrial policy are direct budget and revenue items, any policy requires MOF approval. Japanese industrial policy uses such tools as selective tax measures, access to low-cost government lending, expenditure subsidies, tariff and customs policies, and foreign exchange rate changes. Since every ministry has a corresponding set of program objectives and expenditures, MOF's budgeting sets the limits on the scope of industrial policy and approves its financial particulars. Its perspective is broad, but its scrutiny can be very narrow; accordingly, MOF senior officials examine industrial policy proposals at several levels. They are concerned with the soundness of the national currency as well as with specific loans to business and with adequate government revenue generation as well as with tax subsidies to particular sectors.

The MOF has seven bureaus—Budget, Tax, Financial, Banking, International Finance, Customs and Tariffs, and Securities—and all can figure prominently in industrial policymaking. Budget and Tax are self-explanatory. The Financial Bureau manages the Fiscal Investment and Loan Plan (FILP), which channels government trust funds into industrial sectors via public corporations that offer loans and grants. These public corporations include the Japan Development Bank, Japan Highway Corporation, and the Export-Import Bank, among others—equal to one half the government's general account budget.[3] The FILP is a major government lever on cash flow in the economy.

The Banking Bureau exercises extraordinary control over both the Bank of Japan and the commercial banking system; together with the Securities Bureau, it gives the ministry considerable influence over investment behavior in the high debt sectors of the economy.

The International Finance Bureau is responsible for international payments and currency exchange. The Japanese have learned from the West Germans how to use exchange rate appreciation as an instrument of industrial policy, forcing industry restructuring and holding down inflation.

Customs and Tariffs is the most conservative bureau in a generally conservative ministry. Over the last ten years, Japan has dismantled its once elaborate tariff and quota system until protection is now at a level comparable to that in the United States and in Western European nations; within Customs and Tariffs, however, the execution of this more liberal policy can be reluctant or even obstructionist.

In preparing the budget for Diet approval, the MOF must match funds to priorities across the whole economy, not just the industrial sector. This constraint is often overlooked by the ardent critics of Japan, Inc., who see the various ministries in conspiracy to promote Japanese manufactures. In fact, for a number of reasons, it has become increasingly difficult to persuade MOF of the merits of programs which favor the business sector. Since the 1975 depression, the budget deficit has grown intolerably large, making tax reliefs and subsidies to industry harder to justify. Other priorities like social insurance and the environment are taking larger shares of budget expenditures and tax relief measures.

Ministry of International Trade and Industry. MITI is the most important institution in Japan's industrial policymaking process. Formed in 1949 by the combination of the Ministry of Commerce and Industry and the Board of Trade, it includes all but a few major industries in its jurisdiction. MITI is notable for the variety of roles it plays—broad policy architect, *ad hoc* working-level problem-solver, formal regulator, regional policy arbiter, and informal administrative guide. In some industries it has a strong statutory authority, in others only a broad and sometimes weak influence.

[3] See Chalmers Johnson, *Japan's Public Policy Companies* (Washington, D.C.: American Enterprise Institute for Public Policy Research, 1978).

Other ministries play roles similar to MITI's in some major industries. Telecommunications producers and Nippon Telephone and Telegraph Corporation are supervised by the Ministry of Posts and Telecommunications. The Ministry of Transport oversees railway equipment producers and operating companies. Pharmaceuticals, one of Japan's developing industries, responds to the Ministry of Health and Welfare. These industrial ministries are in general more conservative and protective internationally of their constituents than MITI is today.

But MITI's influence is pervasive in shaping overall Japanese industrial policy. The ministry has been assigned responsibility for:

(1) Shaping the structure of industry and adjusting dislocations that arise in transition;
(2) Guiding the healthy development of industries and their production and distribution activities;
(3) Managing Japan's foreign trade and its commercial relations;
(4) Ensuring adequate raw materials and energy flows to industry; and
(5) Managing particular areas such as small business, patents, industrial technology, etc.

The breadth of this charter, in both function and spirit, gives MITI a comprehensive perspective across industries and policy areas.

MITI has responsibility for developing industries as well as regulating their excesses. Difficult tradeoffs are made and various policies integrated informally within one ministry culture. Thus it considers the whole range of potential government measures—tax, anti-trust, special lending, price and capacity controls, export and import measures, environmental regulations, raw material price setting and procurement, technology subsidy, dislocation subsidy, regional policy—which influence an industrial sector's performance and its effect on other sectors.

MITI does not employ all these tools in every industry nor does it act independently of other agencies. In fact the treatment of various industries differs enormously; many experience little or no special "policy intervention" for long periods while a few (like petroleum refining and computers) are highly coordinated or subsidized. Moreover, MITI is neither autonomous in determining policy nor can it directly finance its own program. The Fair Trade Commission limits MITI's structural initiatives, the Diet and Prime Minister's office circumscribe MITI politically, and MOF passes judgment on its budgets. MITI, nevertheless, remains the focal point in industrial policy determination, lending it continuity and consistency. There is no pretension of zero-base budgeting,[4] no sudden upheavals after elections. Policy changes are usually a long time coming (which is sometimes a weakness) but well-rooted when they emerge.

Much of the leverage MITI and other agencies exert over industry stems from the pervasive practice of administrative guidance. Administrative guidance occurs when government officials guide industries and firms in desired directions by informal means and without statutory authority. Ministries justify the practice by invoking the broad statutory mandate of laws under which they were established, which call on the ministries to promote, regulate, and guide those industries under their jurisdiction. Japanese academic thinking leans toward the view that specific statutory authority is not required for administrative guidance.[5] Ministerial officials summon representatives of a firm, an industry, or the industry association to their offices and express their wishes or expectations. These may be expressed in the form of a request, a recommendation, or, occasionally, an admonition. Compliance is technically voluntary, but the officials do not hesitate to use the various carrots and sticks available to them—which are often totally unrelated to the issue at hand—to assert their will.

Administrative guidance is a fundamental part of the government-business relationship in Japan. Businessmen generally understand that in the long term it is in their best interest, even though on particular occasions the issue being pressed by the ministry is an unpopular one. MITI, for example, will suggest that a company participate in an unappealing foreign investment project or delay a capacity addition to accomplish a broader end. Firms vary in their rate and spirit of compliance, but all regard administrative guidance as justifiable and part of the price business pays for the valuable services of an economic bureaucracy that in general guides the economy well.

MITI's structure is well-suited to its broad policy role. The Minister's Secretariat and four bureaus—Industrial Policy, International Trade Policy, International Trade Administration, and Industrial Location and Environmental Protection—develop and coordinate policy across industries. Three bureaus—Basic Industries

[4] A budgetary revaluation process which assumes that all items must be re-justified each accounting period.

[5] See Dan Fenno Henderson, *Foreign Enterprise in Japan, Law and Politics,* (Chapel Hill: University of North Carolina Press, 1973).

(steel, chemicals, fertilizer, etc.), Machinery and Information Industries, and Consumer Products Industries—develop programs, implement general policy, and solve problems at the individual industry level. Finally, there are nine regional bureaus that reconcile policy to local issues and develop MITI's extraordinary data base on its industries. The acuteness and soundness of MITI policy are attributable to the interplay among these horizontal policy bureaus and vertical industry bureaus, with their broad powers, comprehensive data base, and first-rate career staff. Japan has thus far avoided the proliferation of layered agencies that single issue politics has brought to America's industrial policy.

The Industrial Policy Bureau has played the major role in guiding overall industrial development. It is this bureau that has emphasized the shift toward more knowledge-intensive businesses. Within the bureau general divisions work out actual policy details: the Industrial Structure Division projects the desired future structure of industrial output and designs broad measures toward achieving it; the Business Behavior Division studies tax measures and labor issues; the Price Policy Division is responsible for seeing that appropriate industries are adequately financed. This last division makes recommendations on which businesses and projects gain access to low interest funds through MOF's Fiscal Investment and Loan Plan.

The Industrial Structure Division does the staff work on basic structure policy. The five explicit criteria used in their deliberations are:

(1) The rate of growth the industrial sector is capable of sustaining, given financial, labor, and other direct constraints;
(2) The desirable structure of the industrial sector in terms of input-output balance, socioeconomic limits like regional balance and environmental protection, the need for productivity increases, etc.;
(3) International competitiveness;
(4) Corporate vitality, particularly adequate profitability and reinvestment rates; and
(5) The optimal rate of structural change which would meet economic targets while keeping dislocations tolerable.

A number of advantages accrue to MITI's organization. MITI officials can negotiate solutions to a problem intramurally, where there is "give and take" on both sides. An example is MITI's adjustment in the metal flatware industry, hit hard by yen revaluation in the late 1970s. Steel is a major cost element to this industry, but flatware is a small customer to steel producers. MITI was able to negotiate raw material price relief for the flatware industry and make it up to the steel companies somewhere else. The more issues under a ministry's jurisdiction, the greater potential for consistent and rational policy, but also a higher quality of staff will be demanded. The staff of MITI based in Tokyo itself is remarkably small—fewer than 2,500 professionals. The small ministry size and its broad range of responsibilities give its professionals a breadth of experience and close relations with one another.

PRIVATE INSTITUTIONS. The MOF and MITI are the center of a web of organizations that influence industrial policy; many of these are not part of government, but include associations of senior businessmen, large trade associations, and large commercial banks.

Business Management Associations. There are four major associations of senior businessmen that seek to influence policy. The Keidanren (Federation of Economic Organization) is the major political voice for big business interests in Japan. Its membership includes some 700 large corporations, a number of important public corporations, and the major industry associations. Keizai Doyukai (Committee for Economic Development) is a somewhat more progressive group, focusing on the role of business in broader issues. Shoko Kaigisho (Chamber of Commerce and Industry) speaks for small businesses in Japan. Its membership includes hundreds of thousands of companies in manufacturing, finance, distribution, etc. Nikkeiren (Japanese Federation of Employers Association) attempts to develop a common labor policy for big business. Its membership is similar to that of Keidanren. The influence of these four federations stems from their comprehensive membership, their skilled permanent staff, and their connection with politicians. Their leadership—known as the Zaikai—communicates directly and effectively with Diet members, taking advantage of the "old school tie" network and the permissive laws governing political contributions. Keidanren acts as a major funnel of campaign contributions to the Liberal Democratic Party, a coalition of small business (tradesmen and farmers) and corporate interests.

Business retains influence in Japan (apart from the fact that its opponents are not yet well-organized and financed) partly because it recognizes the importance of being able to influence government policy; it preserves its influence by keeping issues within the traditional channels. Ezra F. Vogel notes:

> Perhaps the most important factor in influencing industrial policy is the framing of questions about a particular issue within Keidanren as well as MITI. The issues raised thus become the focus of official and unofficial concern and debate. Keidanren has a sizable staff doing research for committee sessions in which business leaders study, debate, and reach decisions about important issues. Government bureaucrats, scholars, and other knowledgeable persons frequently testify before these committees. Formal votes on important issues are almost never taken. Perhaps there is no better phrase to describe this process than consensus building.[6]

Industry Associations. Unlike the business organizations, industry associations are concerned with policy toward individual sectors; they maintain a working relationship with MITI's industry bureaus and divisions. These organizations are far more than data-collecting and lobbying groups. They put forward proposals for MITI policy toward an industry and typically implement the policies that are adopted. Japan's Anti-monopoly Law, for instance, permits MITI to authorize and supervise cartels that operate through these associations. These cartels are limited in duration and must serve specific purposes such as:

(1) Long-term rationalization of production (used effectively in bearings and car parts industries);
(2) Orderly reduction of excess capacity (currently being tried in some heavy process industries such as aluminum);
(3) Promotion of vertical integration (currently being tried in small downstream textile companies);
(4) Short-term production allocation (used frequently in recessions in the heavy process sector, such as chemicals and steel); and
(5) Export price floors during trade crises (historically used in textiles, steel, and other industries).

The tradition of strong trade associations dates from the prewar period when government essentially ran industry through this

[6] Ezra F. Vogel, "Guided Free Enterprise in Japan," *Harvard Business Review*, May/June 1978.

mechanism. The structure remains much the same today, but the functioning is less one-sided. Officers of the associations sit on formal MITI advisory councils attached to the industry bureaus. Considerable data are passed to MITI through informal contact in Tokyo and in regional offices. It is because MITI is exceptionally well-informed at the working level that the much discussed government-business communication can work so well. Once again, government prefers to deal with organizations which can focus constituents' interests, speak conclusively for them, and implement policy once it is reached. Splinter interest groups fighting for support through the media are anathema to the ministry.

City Banks. The thirteen large commercial banks ("city banks") extend one quarter of all loans and discounts made by financial institutions, public and private, in Japan. Their principal borrowers are large corporations. City banks have more interest today in industrial policy than ever before, since it is Japan's more troubled businesses—the heavy process sector, marginal producers in mature manufacturing industries, and a number of trading companies— that are their largest borrowers. Japanese business has traditionally used loans rather than equity to finance its high growth rate. But today it is the competitively vulnerable businesses which have large loans outstanding and not the strong, self-financing companies. The ministries and the banks discuss and study issues together closely, often setting up *ad hoc* committees to examine specific problems.

Moreover, the large banks are linked with the government through the Bank of Japan. The Bank, supervised by MOF, lends money to the thirteen city banks that in turn lend to major Japanese industries. MOF can exert considerable leverage over the banks, and on occasion will suggest which projects to support. The banks, although privately owned, rarely resist. Such a relationship helps both parties: the ministries occasionally need the assurance of funds for their client industries, and the Bank's portfolio sometimes needs government assistance to remain sound.

Thus a number of common interests, as well as more direct financial or political ties, link these quasi-public institutions to the government policymaking bodies. Considerable tensions, of course, exist between the government agencies whose concern is Japan's overall international competitiveness and business associations organized to protect their own interests. But there is a process to resolve them.

POLICY OBJECTIVES

The process of selecting structural objectives and reconciling them to limited resources is enormously complex and, if not grounded in good data and real understanding of industry competition and producers' behavior, can generate absurd policies. The Japanese approach reconciles relatively well the macroeconomic aspects of sector shifts, as well as productivity and output targets, with the microeconomic questions of whether company cash flow will be high enough to finance necessary growth and whether Japan can compete internationally in certain business areas, given the industry structure. This of course is where the central economic planner can often fail.

Japan's industrial policy process is often misunderstood. In sectors of policy interest, MITI collects a good deal of market and competitive data, gives administrative guidance to firms, and issues a lot of paper in support of a policy. Communication between MITI and individual producers takes place frequently and at several levels. Some observers of this process have mistakenly concluded that MITI is dictating investment rates in the industry. This is not MITI's intention. Market prospects, not ministries, stimulate investment in growth businesses and ultimately discourage investment in declining ones. MITI understands that it would be counterproductive to force wary producers to invest. Nor can a ministry know any particular business sector well enough to design or direct a specific series of investments. Instead, MITI tries to develop a shared perception of a business's future and designs incentives and subsidies to accelerate the desired course.

Nor does MITI normally have the power to dictate investment choices to business. Indeed the autonomy of the individual firm sharply limits the government's ability to change industrial structure. What is industry development for MITI is risky capital investment for the firm, which although interested in sector structure is more directly interested in its competitive position. Unless its survival is at stake, a company will accept the incentives and subsidies available to the industry, but balk at measures that threaten its autonomy. For example, in the 1960s, Japan's motor car companies welcomed the government's import protection, low-cost lending, and tax deferrals, but rejected MITI's attempts to merge producers and keep minority foreign capital investment out of the industry. In the 1970s the key mainframe computer producers—Hitachi, Fujitsu, and Nippon Electric—remained independent competitors despite MITI attempts to consolidate the industry. In electronic calculators, Sharp and others successfully deflected MITI's attempt to shut off U.S. integrated circuit imports, which threatened Japan's fledgling high-cost production. While serving MITI's longer-term structural aims, this import ban would have seriously damaged calculator producers' cost position. More recently, aluminum producers have resisted MITI's plan for permanent capacity retirement by formula allocation. The producers want short-term relief only in order to preserve long-term strategy flexibility.

Although conflicts do arise between MITI and reluctant companies, the ministry has many tools of persuasion. It has carrots—it can provide access to funds for investment—and it has sticks: it can hold up building permits, regulate raw material imports, and provide material incentives to competitors. However, MITI's greatest strength appears to be its understanding of the competitive stages through which an industry moves and its ability to fashion appropriate policy.

MITI's policy objectives vary according to the competitive position of a business. For businesses in the early, rapid growth phases of development, such as computers and machinery, policy calls for protection from foreign competition among producers, government support of the industry's cash flow, and stimulation of new technology. Today, real protection is available only to a few industries, but MITI remains aggressive on the other fronts. For businesses which are already internationally competitive—motor cars, steel, consumer electronics—government assistance recedes[7] as it is no longer necessary. Finally, for businesses in competitive decline, MITI becomes active again, this time trying to bring about capacity reduction and rationalization.

The process of discussion and debate between MITI and the companies in response to developments in the market place creates a dynamic decision-making process. MITI aptly refers to Japan as a "plan-oriented market economy."

POLICY CONCERNS AND POLICY INSTRUMENTS

There are three broad industrial policy concerns of MITI and the other industrial ministries—investment rate and structure of

[7]With the significant exception of occasional officially sanctioned recession and export cartels coordinated by the industry associations.

producers, technology development, and export-import measures. A general survey of measures brought to bear on these concerns is now presented.

Investment Rate and Structure of Producers. Japan has adopted policies generally favorable to capital investment: no capital gains tax on securities, central bank permanent control of interest rates, a strong anti-inflation commitment, and a minimum of administrative barriers. A relatively high growth rate in the economy as a whole also helps sustain high investment.

MITI, however, does not always favor investment by all competitors. In the rapid-growth development stage of an industry, MITI prods an industry to concentrate; conversely, in no-growth declining sectors, MITI promotes capacity retirement. In both cases MITI's objective is to accelerate market forces and bring about more stable competition among a few relatively low cost producers. In Japan the key concern has been putting capital together, not splitting it apart.

Historically, the government has protected rapid growth industries from imports with formal barriers at the same time that it has sought to eliminate marginal producers. The success of these consolidation efforts has been mixed. MITI exercised strong authority in the most fragmented industries, like sewing machines and car parts, where concentration brought unquestioned benefits in larger scale and lower costs. But in industries where marginal producers were still large companies—motor cars, petroleum refining, and chemicals—MITI failed to bring about mergers and absorptions. Group banks provided easy access to low-cost capital while high growth concealed weaknesses and postponed the shakeout. MITI has usually managed to enforce a capacity expansion queue in the capital-intensive, heavy process industries, in part through foreign exchange control of their raw materials. Even here, however, mavericks like Idemitsu in refining and Sumitomo in steel have been able to elude control.

Today, only a handful of fast growth, high technology industries, such as computers, telecommunications, and railway equipment, are protected from imports, and primarily through closed procurement rather than duties and quotas. In telecommunications and railway equipment, investment is stimulated and competition allocated directly by operating public corporations that buy the equipment.

There is open competition, however, among Japanese computer producers, and government has done its utmost to support investment in this business. It finances most leasing and software to preserve the producers' capital. The Japan Development Bank grants low interest loans to producers to finance the generation of new equipment. And the tax laws generously cushion producers from the loss on the trading in of old machines; accelerated depreciation of capital investment is also given. MITI has tried for years to consolidate the mainframe industry into two or three equipment-compatible groups, but centrifugal forces have prevailed. Six Japanese mainframe manufacturers remain, and even given the increased rationalization among them, they divide the market very thinly. Fujitsu and Hitachi, the two leaders after International Business Machines (IBM), together have less than 40 percent of the total market.

As it encourages investment and formally or informally protects knowledge-intensive growth industries, MITI discourages investment in and protection of declining industries. Today some large declining industries—aluminum smelting, shipbuilding, synthetic textile fibers, etc.—pose major structural problems. These industries are high cost internationally, have excess capacity, and have large outstanding loans.

In May 1978 the Diet passed the Structurally Depressed Industries Law, enabling MITI to develop a stabilization plan using government funds. The procedure specified by the law is typically Japanese. Industries become eligible for assistance only if two thirds of the producers petition MITI, which then decides whether to grant their request. This condition helps the ministry to bring about a working agreement among the producers, whose cost positions and proposed solutions usually differ significantly. The major creditors like the Industrial Bank of Japan sit on *ad hoc* committees with MITI to study the nature of the problem in a particular industry and ways to solve it. The law establishes a government loan guarantee fund when the producers borrow heavily because of massive scrapping or mothballing of capacity.

Concerns for industry structure and investment will occur in growth and decline phases only. In both cases, industry consolidation at optimal scale is the major goal. Currently competitive industries receive little attention.

Technology Development. A second concern of Japanese industrial policy is technology development. This concern has grown as Japan has moved toward more knowledge-intensive industries and as it has approached the frontiers of technology. There are some major government financing efforts—notably in energy and semiconductors—

but the government mainly uses a variety of incentives for private development.

The government's own research and development effort is small, in part because the Japanese have been so successful in exploiting the basic research of American and European government and university laboratories, and in part because large national applied research projects are managed by government laboratories but performed on contract by working groups of corporations. MITI's Agency of Industrial Technology has sixteen associated research institutes that organize and manage long-term large-scale projects to develop system technologies for commercial use. Some current examples are VLSI semiconductors, high performance jet engines, water desalination, and natural resource recycling. These projects run for five to eight years, can cost hundreds of millions of dollars, and are typically performed and co-funded by *ad hoc* associations of several large corporate and university laboratories. They are exempt from the anti-monopoly law.

For industry in general, government uses a variety of more modest incentives and supporting tools for corporate research and development. These include tax credits, grants, loans, and sponsorship of associations. Some are available to all corporations while others are tied to particular MITI objectives.

There are three principal corporate tax incentives for technology development. One stipulates that 25 percent of any year-to-year increase in research and development expenditures over the previous year is a tax credit, up to a limit of 10 percent of total corporate tax. In 1978, manufacturing companies realized a 15 billion yen benefit through this credit. The second is accelerated depreciation on research and development facilities and hardware, which can often mean a 60 percent write-off of the original purchase price in the first year. The provisions try to conserve the cash flow of high technology businesses. As growth of an industry slows, these incentives, appropriately enough, become ineffective, and more cash flow is exposed to tax. The third is a lower tax rate on income received from technology licensed overseas—worth 10 billion yen to the manufacturing sector in 1978.

The government, in cooperation with other institutions, also directly funds research and development. Such grants can take one of several forms. Most common is a matching grant. Ministries receive applications in designated research and development areas from either companies or associations formed for that purpose. Many associations are groups of small companies that could not finance new technologies on their own. Often the technology issue is straightforward: for example, developing a continuous textile operation to replace a vertically fragmented one. For small business, MITI or the trade association sponsors these arrangements. Matching programs are not, however, a major funding source of Japanese corporate research and development; they typically account for less than one percent of the total. A parallel matching grant program is run separately for small business.

Motor car and boat racing tax proceeds also benefit research and development. MITI guides the direction of these funds to various industry associations, which then distribute the money to specific projects in rationalization, research, and export promotion. They are separate from the government's official budgets and help to finance sectors and products that are not household words in Japan. In 1978, racing subsidies to the machinery industries, for example, were 7.3 billion yen.

Loans for technology development form a traditional element of Japanese industrial policy. The Japan Development Bank makes loans under various program headings—commercialization of new technology, developments of prototypes, and commercialization of new technology for small enterprise. These loans are project-related and represent simply low-cost funds—hence they are a marginal incentive. Loans are provided primarily to manufacturers and sometimes to users of the qualifying machinery. These programs have grown throughout the 1970s. The government lent a total of 30 billion yen to all Japanese industry in 1976.

Overall, the government has increased its commitment to research and development over the decade rather substantially, mainly in the form of a few large high-priority projects. This is consistent with the restructuring toward more knowledge-intensive industries.

Export-Import Measures. The third major concern of Japanese industrial policy has been international trade. Through the early 1970s, the Japanese government stimulated exports, restricted manufactured imports, and assisted large-scale raw material imports—classical behavior for an island economy poor in natural resources and prone to experience trade deficits. The tax system, through special reserves and accelerated depreciation, effectively shielded significant portions of export revenue from taxation. The Bank of Japan discounted short-term export bills at less than market interest rates, and cheap long-term credit for export-related investment was available from the Japan Development Bank and the Long

Term Credit Bank of Japan. High duties and quotas blocked imported manufacturers where Japan thought itself uncompetitive. Assistance was given to overseas projects in mining, forestry, and the like, with financial guarantees and government-to-government assurances in order to strengthen supply security in basic materials.

The story is quite different now. Broad export incentives are gone. The tax system retains incentives only for exports by small and medium-size companies and for overseas investment. Export-related accelerated depreciation—worth 55 billion yen to the manufacturing sector in 1970—was eliminated in 1972. Export bills now carry only a quarter of one percent discount off domestic bill rates, and this subsidy works primarily to bolster Japan's declining exporters of textiles, plywood, flatware, etc.

Although MITI no longer directly assists exports, certain government policies and practices do aid selected knowledge-intensive industries. Japan's Export-Import Bank aggressively finances and insures exports of plant systems—a rapidly growing part of trade. Large Third World development projects that Japan finances and supplies enjoy top priority and receive official economic aid. The country's utility monopolies in power generation and telecommunications protect and support designated key products and provide a large production volume on which to base an export effort.

The Japanese home market for manufactures is now essentially open, and foreign producers' market penetration depends on marketing effort and the suitability of the product far more than government-approved barriers. There are three major exceptions to this pattern. One is government-operated monopolies, such as telecommunications, railway, cigarettes, and some computers. Closed procurement is the tool. Ministries other than MITI typically oversee these barriers and are under considerable international pressure to liberalize them. The second relates to machinery imports, where the structure of Japanese industry keeps imports to a minimum. Heavy industry companies are often part of large Zaibatsu[8] containing chemical, steel, electrical equipment, and other companies which exercise closed buying.

The other exception is Japan's political wards like agriculture, retailing, and unskilled labor-intensive manufacturing, where large, competitively vulnerable constituencies command protection. This residual protection is similar to that in other advanced countries. By and large, however, the appreciation of the yen and the migration of

[8]Large industrial groups or conglomerates are known as Zaibatsu.

labor-intensive production to developing countries is opening the door to imports. A large number of Japanese industries—textiles, aluminum, chemicals, and metal working—are under increasing pressure as international product specialization shapes trade patterns.[9]

SOME MYTHOLOGY

Any summary description of the Japanese approach to industrial policy runs the risk of becoming a caricature; it is easy to exaggerate the regularity of the processes, the unanimity of decisions, and the economic rationality of policies. The Japanese government is not a monolith in industrial matters. Even in Japan, budgetary politics and open rivalry among ministries can make policy consensus difficult to achieve and sometimes impossible. And here, as elsewhere, excessive zeal sometimes induces shortsightedness.

When a policy issue cuts across the ties that bind the policy-making groups together, consensus is difficult—sometimes impossible—to achieve. A vigorous debate on the introduction of a value-added tax has pitted big business, which favors it, against low-profit small business, which prefers the income tax. The ruling Liberal Democratic Party, with both groups as major constituents, is thus divided on the matter. The net effect has been to delay the introduction of the new tax. Similarly, the crisis in the shipbuilding industry has posed the issue of rescuing some significant shipbuilders—a course favored by some senior elected officials, but opposed by the ministries and many bankers. Despite the passage of the Structurally Depressed Industries Law, the industry's structural problems remain unresolved. The consensus building process here is a slow one, but because opposing bodies characteristically overlap on a broad range of issues, eventual orderly compromise is possible.

Moreover, ministries often disagree with one another about policy priorities. MITI has accused the Ministry of Forestry and Agriculture of prolonging unnecessarily its support of food subsidies and import barriers, causing the government to throttle back on expansionist fiscal policies toward the manufacturing sector. MITI opposes the Ministry of Posts and Telecommunications' extremely protectionist attitude toward the domestic telephone exchange equipment industry. Indeed MITI has for some time argued

[9]See James C. Abegglen and Thomas M. Hout, "Facing Up to the Trade Gap with Japan," *Foreign Affairs*, Autumn 1978.

against what it sees as excessive protectionism in other agencies. Finally, in the early postwar period, the Bank of Japan and MITI disagreed on whether Japan should develop its own passenger car industry. MITI, looking ahead to higher value-added industries, favored such a development while the Bank, seeking to conserve the scarce foreign exchange that would be needed for imported technology and capital goods in the short run, opposed it. We are daily reminded who won that battle.

Finally, it is easy to credit the industrial policy process with too much of the responsibility for the country's economic success. MITI has not always been right. For too long, for instance, it doubted the sound basis for Sony's fascination with the transistor and instead defended investments in vacuum tubes. No analysis of government's various interventions should overshadow the competence and energy of Japanese corporations and the intense level of competition in most domestic markets. In fact, many of Japan's very successful, internationally dominant industries, such as consumer electronics, motorcycles, and copiers, are ones in which domestic competition has been especially high—without a significant government role.

The following three chapters present six case studies illustrating Japanese industrial policy and its evolution from the issues of the 1950s through those of the present day. We examine the history of industry development and government-business interaction in two generally successful industries—steel and motor cars; in two troubled, declining industries—aluminum and shipbuilding, and in two industries which are just coming into international prominence—industrial machinery and information electronics.

IV

JAPANESE STEEL AND MOTOR CAR INDUSTRIES

The first two case studies concern Japanese industries which are currently international leaders in the products they manufacture—steel and motor cars.[1] The studies document the government policies which helped these industries to develop, through both crisis and expansion. It also demonstrates how, once the ability to compete internationally was achieved, the government's role receded sharply. Particularly interesting is the ability of MITI to apply a precise, light touch to a problem. MITI's policy initiatives generally recognize the varying economic requirements for success in different businesses. Interesting, too, are the conflicts among the ministries and between a particular ministry and the industry. Most conflicts are resolved through an orderly process and are eventually translated into effective action. A few problems—like MITI's attempt to consolidate the motor car industry—remain unsolved.

THE STEEL INDUSTRY

The Japanese steel industry is the world's third largest in tonnage output behind the USSR and the United States. It is, however, the world's most efficient. Several major studies, public and private, over the last few years have indicated that the Japanese are significantly lower cost producers of the normal range of basic carbon steel products than any other major producer. Even the American Iron and Steel Institute has acknowledged that the Japanese have a 15 percent productivity advantage over U.S. producers.

Steel is traditionally the *sine qua non* of industrial development and military strength. Accordingly, governments have always kept a close watch over their steel industries. Some countries, including many in Europe and the Third World, have fully nationalized their

[1]The discussion in this chapter draws significantly on earlier published Boston Consulting Group case studies in *Japan: The Government—Business Relationship* (Washington D.C.: U.S. Department of Commerce, 1972).

steel industries while others, like the United States, have limited the government role to a careful monitoring of the industry's pricing.

The Japanese government has played a supportive role in its steel industry and has derived a great deal of influence from its actions. Steel in Japan is not government owned, and competition is considerable among major producers. But the results have been very much in the public interest—low cost steel inputs to other manufacturing industries, a major source of foreign exchange, and reasonably viable steelmaking companies.

Japan's policy toward the industry over the last thirty years illustrates the characteristic flexibility and attention to competitive business economics of its industrial policy in general. In the late 1940s, the government identified steel as crucial to Japanese reindustrialization and took immediate measures to restore prewar production capability. Beginning in the late 1950s and 1960s, steel received special priority as a key feeder industry to shipbuilding, motor cars, domestic appliances, and other capital-intensive industries. By the early 1970s, Japan's steel industry had achieved world dominance and could be considered self-sustaining. Government assistance to the industry therefore virtually disappeared. Today, despite its continued preeminence worldwide, the industry is understood to be entering its declining phase, and MITI is discouraging domestic investment, promoting rationalization in the industry, and supporting steel investment abroad.

Throughout this evolutionary process, three basic forms of assistance have been at the heart of Japanese policy: financing to build new plants, assistance in procurement of scarce raw materials necessary for growth, and assistance with cash flow during recessions.

CAPACITY EXPANSION

Financing. Steel is an extremely capital-intensive industry, with an assets-to-sales ratio exceeding 1.5 to 1. Over time, as the optimum scale of steel plants and of individual mills has risen, the cost of building new greenfield plants has increased enormously. As discussed in Chapter II, U.S. steel companies have not been able to justify the construction of new greenfield plants on a return-on-investment basis, and instead have tended to add capacity and make modernization investments in a less efficient, roundout fashion. The Japanese pursued a very different course. In a climate of rapid domestic demand growth, companies incurred extremely high debt-to-equity ratios and made the investments needed to build the new greenfield plants.

Immediately after the war the Reconstruction Finance Bank, a government financial institution, provided most of the capital for rehabilitating the industry. The government subsidized the steel price level to help the relatively inefficient industry begin to rebuild its markets. In the early 1950s, MITI developed the first rationalization plan for the industry: industry growth was to be promoted through both tax incentives and financing assistance.

The tax measures applicable to the steel industry were proposed by a study group within the Ministry of Finance after examination of the tax systems of other nations. Five tax and duty exemptions were enacted in 1951-52:

(1) Import duty exemption on designated steel-making equipment (60 percent of such equipment was imported at the time);
(2) Fifty percent increase in depreciation base allowed on designated equipment;
(3) Tax exemption for reserves meant to cover price changes in inventories and securities;
(4) Tax exemption for revaluation of assets, which effectively increased the depreciation base; and
(5) Tax exemption for additional bad debt reserves.

These measures increased the funds available for reinvestment and, in particular, for investment in optimum scale facilities embodying "state-of-the-art" technology. Between 1951 and 1955, about one quarter of all capital investment originated internally, primarily through these tax exemptions.

The greater part of investment capital—roughly 65 percent—was financed by debt, primarily through government financial institutions, although supplemented by private financial institutions. Loans from the Japan Development Bank and the Long Term Credit Bank (both government owned) and the Industrial Bank of Japan (government influenced) accounted for roughly half of the $95 million in debt incurred by the steel industries during the period. The government encouraged commercial banks to finance steel expansion, and the Ministry of Finance permitted $11 million of foreign exchange loans to the industry.

The first rationalization plan (1951-1954) doubled Japanese crude steel production from 4.8 to 9.5 million tons. Equally noteworthy was the nature of the government's involvement in this process. MITI avoided the role of direct central planner and concentrated instead on mobilizing financial resources and creating financial incentives for growth. Government banks and private financial institutions were persuaded to provide funds to the industry, but final judgments on specific borrowers and amounts were left to the banks, particularly among the commercial banks. The tax measures also helped direct investment appropriately without overt government dictation. The reserve and special depreciation measures favored growing firms at the expense of stagnant firms, and steered investment toward designated types of equipment.

Between 1955 and 1960 a second rationalization plan, embodying similar measures, produced another doubling of capacity. This pattern continued throughout the 1960s. Japan's capital/output ratio in steel production (stock of physical capital per ton of steel produced) consistently remained the highest in the world and nearly twice that of the United States during the latter part of the 1960s. In addition, because of the willingness to build greenfield plants, capital could be used more efficiently. Greenfield plants constructed after 1952 produced over 80 percent of Japanese carbon steel production compared to less than 5 percent in the United States.

Throughout the 1960s the role of direct government financing declined, although the government informally encouraged and, in some cases, insured private bank loans to the industry. Since the banks are important stockholders in the companies, they had incentives to continue to lend money. Between 1966 and 1972, the assets of the five largest producers grew at a formidable annual rate of 23 percent, representing a huge amount of capital expenditure. During this critical period, when crude steel production grew from 41 million tons to 100 million tons, the industry sustained a debt-to-equity ratio of almost 12 to 1. By this time, the government did not need to provide much of the funding directly, but it did guarantee much of the lending and in some cases subsidized low interest rates.

Coordination. In addition to assisting in the financing of capacity expansions, the government played a coordinating role in approval of expansion plans. Both government and steelmakers had long recognized that a joint determination of the rate of capacity additions was in both their interests. The impact of steel expansion on the economy, the massive financial requirements, and the difficulties of imbalance in steel demand and supply dictated that the government should influence the rate of growth of capacity. Steelmakers, in turn, were generally willing to cooperate among themselves and with MITI because of the cash flow crises and price instability that follow over-expansion.

The capacity expansion approval process has changed somewhat over time, but it operates roughly as follows: Representatives of the privately owned steel producing firms gather under the umbrella of the Japan Iron and Steel Federation to present and discuss tentative investment plans for the coming year. (Often these representatives, usually managing directors, are MITI alumni.) The producers' plans are evaluated in relation to the demand outlook for the industry and the existing pattern of market shares. After these meetings and informal discussions among these managers and the officials of the Iron and Steel Section of MITI's Heavy Industries Bureau, the presidents of the steel companies try to reach a consensus on the rate and timing of the major investments of individual producers. MITI participates *ex officio* in these meetings. The frequency of consensus meetings varies with the complexity of the problem; in times of crisis, meetings are continuous.

After consensus has been reached, MITI issues a report recommending a course of action to the industry. In recent years this report has been prepared by the Iron and Steel Subcommittee of MITI's Industrial Structure Council, a policy advisory group which reports at the vice-ministerial level. The council's membership includes officials from several ministries including Finance, prominent businessmen, and leading academics.

This process should not be viewed in terms of the Western dichotomy between public and private forces. The government neither plans nor dictates the rate of capacity expansion. The Industrial Structure Council does not unilaterally accept or reject the industry's consensus, but rather evaluates it in view of Japan's wider economic objectives. It has been said that no application from a major firm for a capacity increment has ever been flatly rejected, although some have been delayed. This of course is the mechanism of the consensus process: the expanding firm is persuaded either to delay its application or to accept a delayed approval. When this persuasion fails, consensus is frustrated.

The government can draw on both official and unofficial sources of authority to facilitate consensus. MITI's control over imported raw materials is one crucial policy instrument. Through foreign exchange import quotas, MITI directly controlled the importation and allocation among producers of both ore and coal until 1965, and still retains control over the import of coking coal. Since Japan currently imports 98 percent of its iron ore requirements and 90 percent of its coal needs, this tool gives MITI reasonably effective control over the rate of production, and hence the rate of expansion. Foreign exchange control also permits the Bank of Japan to limit steel producers' foreign borrowing, which has been a source of finance for the Japanese steel industry.

The Bank of Japan and the Ministry of Finance bring another perspective to the discussions regarding steel expansion. While MITI focuses on the relative competitiveness and growth of the Japanese steel industry, the financial authorities share a broader concern with macro economic effects and international payments balances. Hence in 1970 the Bank denied requests for increased foreign borrowings in order to avoid undermining its domestic deflationary policy and depressing the rate of increase in dollar reserves. This forced the delay of capacity additions in the early 1970s.

The steel industry's good relationship with the bureaucracy, and with the broader economic policymaking community in and out of government, has made these negotiations generally successful. Harmony between MITI and the industry, however, is not universal. A case in point is Sumitomo's recalcitrance in the middle 1960s.

Sumitomo is perhaps Japan's most aggressive steelmaker. Since the middle 1950s, the company has achieved better results in profitability, modernity of facilities, export sales, and market share than any of its competitors in the industry. In 1965 Sumitomo challenged the industry consensus recommendation that steelmakers should delay all new investments in rolling facilities except those which replaced existing capacity. It went ahead with a new installation which, while technically a replacement, substantially improved productivity; at the same time, Sumitomo stepped up production while the majority of producers were trying to keep prices stable by moderating production levels. Fuji Steel vigorously protested against Sumitomo's action and comparable aggressive behavior on the part of smaller steelmakers, and argued that only special legislation governing steel investment could resolve the industry's fundamental problem of overcapacity.

Response within MITI was mixed. Many, including the outgoing vice-minister, defended the traditional system of industrial consensus reached under MITI's watchful eye—an arrangement which Sumitomo felt put the fast-growing, efficient steelmakers who were responsible for Japan's international success at a disadvantage. It may be inferred that Sumitomo's view was echoed by the Fair Trade Commission, as it reiterated its disapproval of existing production cartels as anti-competitive. At the other extreme, a study committee of the

Industrial Structure Council used this occasion to argue that the problems of capacity regulation and price stability could best be solved by a thorough consolidation of the steel industry.

The upshot of these confrontations was continuation of the status quo. Sumitomo continued to build its new facilities and produce aggressively. MITI disciplined the company by limiting its allocation of imported coking coal to what it considered appropriate levels. Before Sumitomo really felt the effect of this action, however, demand for steel recovered sharply, and by 1967 Sumitomo's additional capacity was needed to meet domestic requirements.

The Sumitomo incident clearly indicates the limitations of the consensus system. But the majority of industry or government leaders would not have tolerated a more radical form of control. The consensus system struck an acceptable balance between autonomy and control, though this might have been more difficult had demand not recovered.

More recently, as steel has come to be regarded as less important in Japan's future, MITI has begun to discourage major investments at home, and to call for further industry rationalization. As early as 1974, MITI was reluctant to support continued general expansion in the industry in Japan, despite the then current steel boom. Since then, a long-term recession and worldwide overcapacity in steel have confirmed them in this view. Japan's remaining small local open-hearth furnace producers have been designated as a troubled industry and are being encouraged to come up with a long-term plan to reduce capacity. MITI has, however, favored foreign investment by Japanese firms in overseas steel mills, particularly in developing countries, as a way of maintaining Japanese dominance in steel while promoting the growth of the Japanese steelmaking machinery and whole plant export industries. MITI has encouraged Japanese participation in steel projects in Qatar, Iraq, and Saudi Arabia, among others.

In general, then, MITI helped industry growth very directly in the beginning, and more indirectly and informally during the 1960s and early 1970s. Its actions stemmed from a belief that having the largest, most efficient steel industry in the world would be a valuable national asset for many years to come, benefitting many other Japanese industries using steel. Means were found to spread the risk inherent in the commitment of vast financial resources to the industry while still providing a good return on equity for investors in the steel companies.

RAW MATERIAL ACQUISITION

Scale plants alone cannot guarantee a competitive steel industry; low-cost, high-quality raw materials are also essential. Because Japan produces only about 10 percent of its total coking coal needs and almost none of its iron ore needs, ensuring a steady supply of good quality raw materials at a reasonable cost has been a major preoccupation of government policy. Long-term contracts arranged by the steel industry account for roughly four-fifths of the resources consumed in steelmaking itself. The Japanese government has provided a good deal of financial help. Government institutions such as the Export-Import Bank and the Overseas Economic Cooperation Fund directly finance imports. These institutions provide the assurance of long-term financing which is necessary in order to enter into supply agreements with overseas mining operations, many of whose total output and hence total investment is targeted for Japan. In addition to providing a long-term source of funds, the government designates iron ore and coal as priority import categories and ensures that foreign exchange is allocated to purchase them.

The government has also assisted steelmakers in undertaking direct overseas resource development investment. The Ministry of Finance once designated special sources in its annual budget in accordance with a standing policy to favor such overseas investment. During the 1950s and 1960s, when Japan's currently productive resource development projects were undertaken, capital exports of scarce foreign exchange were authorized first for ore, coal, and petroleum exploration and mining ventures. Resource development accounted for 30 percent of total cumulative Japanese foreign investment in 1970.

Just as important as the formal availability of loan funds for development has been the priority the government has given this type of investment and the resulting diverse forms of support. On several occasions MITI's alacrity in directing funds to a Japanese development coordinator, usually a large trading company, has proved critical to the project's success. Similarly, the government can ensure that funds are available for the export of Japanese equipment and technology that usually attends the overseas development project. MITI and the steel companies have dispatched teams of exploration experts to investigate possible coal development sites in Canada and Australia and to advise the developer. The Japan Overseas Development Corporation, a public corporation and a counterpart to the Japan Petroleum Development Corporation, assists in the organization and financing of development projects abroad. The government has unequivocally demonstrated its commitment to develop foreign sources of ore and coal supply.

A third, more minor form of government financial assistance has been tax incentives and insurance against development losses. A contingency reserve for possible losses and thorough development loss insurance facilities are available to overseas ventures.

The government is also supporting basic geological exploration in prospective supply areas. In addition, public funds have established a resource development college to provide professional training in exploration and mining. However, the state has not directly invested in resource development on a significant scale nor does it direct the efforts of manufacturers and trading companies in exploration or mining.

While government's role in assisting capacity addition in the steel industry has declined in recent years, its interest in raw materials acquisition has increased. In the past, although Japanese companies and the government would agree to enter into long-term purchasing contracts for Australian and Brazilian iron ore and U.S., Canadian, and Australian coal, actual Japanese investment in these developments was minimal. Since the 1973 energy and raw material shortages demonstrated that availability (not just the cost) of supply was an issue, Japanese companies, with government assistance, have invested in new mining projects. The increasing strength of the yen and the existence of dollar surpluses have also spurred overseas investment.

In general, the government has not itself invested in these projects or directly provided the funds for investment, but rather has helped to convene consortia and, through MITI's and the Ministry of Finance's involvement in discussions and negotiations, has influenced the direction taken. Government has also contributed to the success of development projects by relaxing antitrust regulations to allow cartels to invest and import raw materials; in some cases, the government has guaranteed financing.

CARTELS

A final kind of government assistance to the steel industry has been the formation of recession cartels and export restraint cartels. Steel production is capital-intensive both in the form of fixed and working capital. Reductions in steel production, leading to under-utilization of capacity, can be extremely damaging, and the cyclical nature of the worldwide steel production has often caused severe cash flow problems for producers. Most American companies, for instance, show great swings in profitability and usually only have funds to invest during boom periods. It requires a few years to build new capacity, which then may come into use at the time of the next recession, thus exacerbating cash flow problems. As a result, producers are often tempted to cut prices in order to maintain capacity utilization; this can compound the industry's problems and distort its long-term growth potential.

This problem first appeared in Japan during the mild recession of 1957, when the country's economic growth faltered in the midst of the steel industry's expansion, creating overcapacity. Because Japan's steelmakers operate with exceptionally high fixed financial and labor costs, and because capacity additions were accelerating, a severe cash flow crisis resulted from substantial under-utilization. Prices dropped as producers tried to restore normal levels of capacity utilization. As the crisis deepened, individual firms began to cut prices drastically.

Self-motivated collusion among firms to restrict production and stabilize prices would have violated the anti-monopoly act. In this impasse, MITI led informal consultations with industry management and developed a public sales system to ameliorate the problem. Under this arrangement, steel producers agreed upon and reported their scheduled monthly production levels to MITI along with price schedules. Prices were made public, and the industry's entire monthly output was to be sold at the announced prices. Thus, without unilaterally setting production limits and price levels, MITI was able to bring producers to an enforceable consensus.

Since the late 1950s, similar means have been used during major recessions to promote an orderly cutback in production and to manage pricing. In normal economic conditions, however, there is no price fixing or price control, and Japanese steel prices have steadily fallen as the industry's productivity and raw material supply have improved.

MITI has also coordinated voluntary export restraint cartels. The Export-Import Transaction Law of 1952 allows exporters to "enter into an agreement with respect to price, quantity, grade, design, and other items in the export business of a designated category of goods to be exported to a specified destination by reporting to MITI," and gives MITI the authority to alter or suspend the agreement if it cannot function effectively or if it fails to serve legitimate purposes.

Such export restraint cartels were organized in the late 1960s in response to pressure from the U.S. government to limit exports of Japanese steel products to the United States.

SPECIALTY STEELS

The most significant government cartel intervention in the industry came in response to the specialty steels crisis brought about by the recession of 1964-65. Specialty steel production—stainless, tool, etc.—grew rapidly from 1960 to 1965, but capacity grew even faster. By 1965, significant overinvestment had occurred. The major source of overinvestment was the entry of additional carbon steel producers into the stainless, tool, and structural alloy fields.

In February 1964 the Japanese government initiated a deflationary monetary policy. As economic growth began to slow down, machinery and motor car producers reduced their steel orders. Specialty steel producers cut prices sharply to maintain market share and plant operating levels, but specialty steel production actually declined from 1964 to 1965.

The industry and MITI responded quickly. MITI suggested guidelines for voluntary production cutbacks as early as April 1964. Demand fell faster than production, however, and by the end of 1964 production cuts of 10 to 15 percent from previous-year levels were necessary. A formal production cartel was organized by MITI in January 1965 for structural alloy steel. In March of the same year a more stringent measure—a price cartel—followed as prices continued to deteriorate. March 1965 also marked the financial collapse of Sanyo Specialty Steel, the largest bankruptcy of the postwar period. In December, MITI organized a production cartel for stainless and bearing steel. The economy recovered in 1966, and by September all cartels were abolished.

During the crisis, MITI took the initiative to push for a reorganization of the industry. The Specialty Steel Policy Subcommittee of the ministry's powerful Industry Structure Deliberation Council recommended a program for reform. In November 1965 the subcommittee issued a report calling for cooperative efforts between MITI and the industry in three areas: vertical rationalization of production among carbon steel and specialty producers, specialization within steelmaking groups of particular products, and formal mergers of competing or complementary producers. Some significant changes were made over the next five years.

The government also acted to rescue individual firms from bankruptcy. Two major producers, Sanyo and Nippon Specialty, slid toward bankruptcy in 1965. Under the Corporate Rehabilitation Act, the government sponsored the reorganization and refinancing of these two firms. MITI, the Ministry of Finance, the Bank of Japan, and the commercial banks all played important roles. In the case of Nippon Specialty Steel, the rehabilitation plan was drawn up in December 1966 by the major creditors and shareholders under the supervision of the Ministry of Finance. In short, the method of rehabilitation was to reduce by large amounts the unsecured debt and paid-in capital without compensation to creditors and shareholders. Under the guidance of the Ministry of Finance, new shares were issued to creditors holding the cancelled debt instruments, mortgaged debt was frozen, and new management was installed. New debt was arranged through the intervention of the Bank of Japan.

In the commodity steel industry, such extensive government intervention has not been needed. Since the early 1970s, government has been working to rationalize existing capacity in commodity steel by enforcing agreements to close the least efficient furnaces during recessions as new ones came onstream and, more recently, by strongly encouraging the rationalization of the small weak competitors. These actions, like those in specialty steels, have come in response to industry crisis and at the request of the companies involved rather than as an imposition from government.

SUMMARY

As discussed in Chapter II, Japan's success in steel can be largely attributed to aggressive investment strategies which allowed the country to build the world's lowest cost steel industry.

The value of government support to the industry cannot be measured in terms of cash expenditures. By the judicious application of support in the areas where it could be most effective, government has done a great deal for the industry. Selective measures—help through the insurance of debt for building greenfield plants, assistance in procuring raw materials and forming anti-recession cartels—have provided support without extinguishing competition or stifling initiative in individual companies. Even capacity expansion cooperation has been carried out in such a way as to allow substantial continued internal competition and even greater market share than occurred in the United States. The actual flow of funds from government to the industry represented by loans, grants, and tax allowances has been minimal, at least since the late 1950s. Per ton of steel, such assistance has been substantially less than that supplied by many European governments (often to subsidize the losses of uncompetitive plants).

THE MOTOR CAR INDUSTRY

The Japanese motor car industry, with two of the world's four largest companies in terms of output, is now second only to the United States in total production, and is the largest exporter of automobiles in the world. The top three foreign cars sold in the United States are Japanese, and this success has come in a comparatively short period of time. In 1965 Japan exported only 100,000 cars, primarily to other Asian countries, and even in 1970 fewer than 700,000 cars were exported. By 1978 exports had risen to more than 3 million units.

The Japanese car manufacturers have remained strong despite the revaluations of the yen and the rapid rise in relative Japanese labor costs over the past decade. In fact, the true potential of the industry has not yet been realized, primarily because of formal and informal import restrictions on Japanese-produced cars, particularly in Europe.

The success of Japan's major car firms—Toyota, Nissan, and Honda—stems mainly from their accomplishments in product design and production process. They have focused on a relatively limited range of chassis and engine types. They have achieved significantly higher levels of product reliability through greater discipline in tolerances and extensive pre-production testing. They designed and built high volume automated facilities which, when operating near capacity, are low cost, and they have gained high volume through the growth of their domestic market and a major effort in marketing abroad.

As in other industries, the lethargy of American and European competitors contributed to Japan's success in the sales of motor cars. Except for Volkswagen, none of the European car manufacturers was willing to parallel Japan's heavy investment in marketing, distribution, and service for the large U.S. market; Detroit was slow to develop a true subcompact alternative car to those being imported, and Volkswagen lagged in replacing "the Beetle." Thus Japanese producers were able to capture a large part of the rapidly growing U.S. small car market.

Finally, the large home market was an important asset to the Japanese car industry, providing rapid initial growth and a proving ground for domestic producers. European producers have recently begun cooperative efforts that have consolidated their own market base and made it possible to amortize investment in research and development and automation over greater volume. Had they taken such steps earlier, they might have posed a more effective deterrent to Japanese producers.

POSTWAR RECONSTRUCTION

The Japanese government's role in the motor car industry began in the 1930s, when for military and foreign exchange reasons the government passed a law that forced the market leaders, General Motors and Ford, out of Japan. After failing to encourage Zaibatsu to enter the industry, the government provided incentives for Toyota and Nissan to do so.

In the immediate postwar period, the car industry was in disarray. Toyota, the largest producer, had to be saved from bankruptcy in 1949 by the Bank of Japan. The Bank opposed development of the industry, but MITI was in favor. The Korean War resolved the issue by creating an export market for Japanese-produced motor cars. Thus in 1952 MITI developed a policy to protect and help fund development of the industry and to help it acquire needed technology.

The government played a significant role in the industry in the 1950s and 1960s. Government intervention in the car industry was characterized by three major policy goals: discouragement of foreign capital in the Japanese industry and protection against car imports, attempts to bring about rationalization of production, and assistance with overseas marketing and distribution expenditure. Recently the Japanese government has played only a minor role to assist in arranging voluntary European export cutbacks and in the industry's research and development program to develop an electrically powered car.

Protection. The government devised a comprehensive and imposing set of protection measures which discouraged foreign investment in the car industry. These laws specified that no repatriation of earnings or capital would be guaranteed from foreign investment in marketing facilities. Repatriation would be guaranteed for investment in production facilities only if it "contributes to the development of the domestic industry."

MITI's purpose was to discourage import marketing investments while leaving the door open for selected joint ventures with foreign producers who had superior car parts technology. Admission of large American and European motor car assemblers was ruled out. Two instruments—quota and tariff—were used to protect the industry. Quotas were applied throughout the mid-1960s, and prohibitively high tariffs through the mid-1970s. The imposition of import quotas and tariffs created for Japanese producers a market opportunity which they were not technologically prepared to exploit. Domestic producers turned out only 4,317 passenger cars in 1951, and these were uncompetitive in price and quality with Western imports. Parts technology and production methods were undeveloped, and most manufacturers agreed with MITI on the necessity of importing foreign technology.

MITI controlled all foreign licensing agreements. To make technology agreements more attractive to the licensor it guaranteed the remittance of royalties from Japan. The policy stipulated, however, that continued remittance would be guaranteed only if 90 percent of the licensed parts were produced in Japan within five years. MITI had struck a compromise. Obtaining operational foreign technology required substantial imports of foreign "value-added" in the form of parts and sub-assemblies. By making remittance conditional on the transfer of parts manufacture to Japan, however, MITI served notice that knock-down imports would be permitted only for a limited period. Domestic manufacturers were thus given additional incentive to develop manufacturing capability for their licensors' parts.

A year after this policy was adopted, six domestic manufacturers had negotiated agreements for knock-down assembly of foreign cars in Japan under license. Of the six, Nissan was the only one then producing passenger cars; Hino, Mitsubishi, and Isuzu were traditional truck manufacturers. MITI approved the applications of these four, while rejecting those of the two others—Fuji Auto (no relation to Fuji Heavy Industries now producing cars) and Nichiei. MITI considered those firms too financially weak to survive, and it did not want a fragmented industry. Nissan and Isuzu cooperated with Austin (U.K.) and Rootes (U.K.) respectively, while Hino cooperated with Renault and Mitsubishi with Willys (U.S.). Toyota and Prince, two of the three major passenger car producers of the period, used domestic know-how exclusively. The four licensees rapidly developed their own technology, with the result that the assembly of European cars in Japan did not last very long. The Isuzu-Rootes agreement was the longest, running until 1964, but producing less than one million dollars in royalties over twelve years.

INDUSTRY RATIONALIZATION. In the past two decades, the government has used a variety of financial assistance programs to aid the car industry. The Japan Development Bank extended reconstruction loans to car producers from 1951 to 1955, financing roughly 9 percent of their total investment. Special accelerated depreciation rates were extended to car producers, permitting rates of up to 50 percent depreciation in the first year. Finally, during the 1950s, direct subsidies amounting to roughly one million dollars were awarded to the Automobile Technology Association, representing manufacturers. After this initial financial assistance, the major investment role played by the government (primarily MITI) was to encourage rationalization, both of the parts industry and of the motor car industry itself.

The car industry has from its inception been highly competitive internally. As a result, MITI has often met opposition from producers when it advocated mergers and associations within the industry. Particularly in the 1960s and 1970s, the limits of MITI's control can be seen clearly.

MITI's attempts at industry rationalization have been most effective in the parts industry, where they had the cooperation of the major car producers; MITI has been least effective among the producers themselves, where competitive rivalries and the unwillingness of inefficient producers to go out of the business have frustrated the ministry's plans.

The Car Parts Industry. The structure of the motor car producing sector in the Japanese economy resembles a series of pyramids, with the products flowing from the bottom to the top. At the top are the vehicle producers—Toyota, Nissan, etc.—which manufacture engines and design and assemble vehicles. Each assembler is supplied by an affiliated group of primary parts manufacturers. These firms, roughly 300 in number, usually sell exclusively to one assembler.[2] The bottom layer comprises the small parts subcontractors who supply, both exclusively and nonexclusively, the primary parts firms. There are several thousand small subcontractors, many of whom are affiliated through ownership, technology agreements,

[2]It should be noted, however, that several large independent parts manufacturers have now emerged.

or simply captive arrangements with primary parts manufacturers or the assemblers themselves.

This system gave the assembler a stable yet elastic source of supply, as demand fluctuations were absorbed by the marginal subcontractor. Labor costs at the subcontract level were usually lower than in the large firm. However, as design improvements required more advanced parts technologies, the system proved to have some serious drawbacks. The chief problem was the large number and small size of the primary parts manufacturers and subcontractors. A low production scale precluded economies of scale and modern production technologies, and the firms were financially weak. Both MITI and the major car producers recognized that the production efficiency and technological progress of the industry would be inhibited if this structure remained.

MITI had taken a serious policy interest in the parts industry since the early 1950s. In 1952 MITI directed budget monies originally allocated to the car assemblers' development to immediate subsidies for specific parts producers. Over the next few years, it recommended that the Japan Development Bank extend long-term credit to large, viable parts suppliers of the four major car producers. At least ten parts manufacturers participated.

In 1956 MITI used a major piece of new legislation to implement a more thorough financial assistance and rationalization program in the parts industry. An Auto Parts Committee including MITI Heavy Industry Bureau officials, presidents of various parts manufacturers trade associations, and senior officers of the Automobile Industry Association, representing the car manufacturers, was formed to coordinate the program. This *ad hoc* committee was responsible for taking the initiative to develop operational programs acceptable to all its constituents and formally proposing them to MITI. The car parts program was planned in five-year intervals and formally lasted until 1971.

The committee worked between 1956 and 1966 to modernize facilities and concentrate production among fewer producers in forty-five of ninety-five parts categories. Mergers, although encouraged, were not explicitly directed. Using criteria heavily influenced by MITI, the committee approved borrowing for large, specialized exporting firms. Within the constraints of the affiliated system, MITI wanted to develop a small group of large, specialized parts firms capable of competing with American suppliers. At one time MITI reportedly suggested that the number of primary parts manufacturers could be reduced to forty-five. (There presently remain over 300.)

The ten-year program from 1956-66 was reasonably successful. Nearly $50 million in low-interest long-term loans were extended by the Japan Development Bank and the Small Business Finance Corporation over the period. Market share concentration occurred and costs were reduced. Price reductions over this period were critically important to Japan's subsequent export penetration of the U.S. market. Annual percentage price reductions from 1960 to 1965 averaged roughly 30 percent.

Despite gains in industry concentration and efficiency, however, the primary parts manufacturers in 1966 remained largely one- or two-product companies. (The criteria used for the advancement of loans had in fact encouraged specialization.) In addition, Japanese parts manufacturers were smaller than their American counterparts. MITI thought that larger, horizontally integrated parts manufacturers would improve Japan's competitive position and would reduce the need for domestic firms to seek foreign technology through joint equity ventures. Consequently, the rationalization program which MITI approved for the third five-year period (1966-71) emphasized horizontal combination, even across affiliated group lines. The government offered financial assistance either to mergers or to jointly established research efforts by parts producers. MITI hoped to create large "unit system" sub-assembly producers, but the program was not successful. Despite annual production growth rates of 25 to 40 percent during this period, which made low-cost, long-term lending sources extremely attractive to these capital-constrained single product companies, borrowings were not heavy and governmental program budgets were not fully utilized.

Nor was the horizontal consolidation phase of the program successful. A number of subcontractors merged into primary parts manufacturers. For example, two large Nissan affiliates in the lighting equipment area merged, and a three-way clutch venture including Toyota and Nissan affiliates was considered. But there was little impact on the primary parts manufacturers who were the real targets of the program. The major reason for the relative failure of MITI's efforts was that the car producers themselves, especially Nissan, were reorganizing their affiliates during this period. This inevitably caused some tensions. The vertical nature of the affiliate system did not easily accommodate the horizontal, total market orientation of the government's program.

Overall, the consolidation and modernization of parts suppliers during the 1950s and 1960s was essential to the emergence of a world competitive industry. It is clear that government played a crucial role in this effort, although its wishes did not always prevail. By the early 1970s the industry had attained competitiveness, and MITI moved to a "hands-off" policy vis-à-vis the parts industry.

Consolidation Efforts. MITI's attempts to rationalize the manufacture of motor cars failed, although they did exert some influence on producers. The history of this interaction gives a good picture of the tensions within Japanese industrial policy formulation.

During the 1950s and 1960s, MITI attempted to consolidate the industry into fewer and larger "groups" of car producers. Although MITI introduced various consolidation plans, the government and the manufacturers never achieved consensus. A number of business combinations (in the form of mergers and cooperative production arrangements) did occur after 1965. These were largely self-motivated, however, and usually consummated by the producers without direct ministry influence. The consolidations were clearly not responses to MITI's several "grouping" plans enunciated during the decade.

To understand MITI's ambitions requires an appreciation of the circumstances of the motor industry. From the introduction of foreign technology in 1952 until 1960, the number of conventional passenger car producers had remained stable, with Nissan and Toyota the dominant firms. In 1960 three more firms—Mitsubishi, Fuji, and Toyo—entered the passenger car business. The combined car market share of Toyota and Nissan dropped from three-quarters to less than one half between 1960 and 1962. Rapid market entry was, of course, to be expected as passenger car demand soared. During 1961, for example, while Toyota and Nissan together lost 11 percent of their market share, their combined sales revenue grew by 38 percent.

MITI viewed this increase in the number of producers with anxiety. In 1953 the ministry had rejected two of six applications for the import of foreign technology. Two years later, MITI suggested that all car producers should develop a prototype People's Car, and then permit MITI to select one design and subsidize its production by the single preferred manufacturer. The hope was that a single popular car which could dominate the market would be developed. The car manufacturers quietly but strongly objected to the single company subsidy concept, and the plan never reached the Diet. This was perhaps the manufacturers' first major resistance to MITI policy.

MITI's interest in the structure of the industry reflected its concern not only for the efficiency of domestic production but also for international competitiveness. Because liberalization of passenger car import quotas was clearly inevitable, Japanese cars quickly had to become competitive in Japanese markets. Resisting imports was also important for developing the export opportunity. Japanese producers has to preempt all domestic market growth in order to gain sufficient production scale and experience to compete in American and, it was hoped, European markets. Either slow domestic growth, excessive product fragmentation, or premature import liberalization could keep the country's motor car producers from reaching competitive parity. MITI viewed this possibility with great concern, and made a series of efforts to consolidate the industry.

Proposed Reorganization of the Industry. At a 1961 meeting of the Industry Structure Advisory Council, MITI proposed that passenger car producers be organized into groups based on the car's basic design type. Three groups—regular passenger cars, minicars, and specialty cars (including sportscars)—were defined. A firm's entire production would be limited to one group, and minimum volumes would have to be met within three years. The objective was to force a concentration of product line and eventually eliminate small producers.

Toyota and Nissan—neither of whom produced minicars—reportedly did not voice strong opposition to the plan, which would have reduced competition in conventional passenger cars. Toyo Kogyo, Mitsubishi, Daihatsu, and Fuji, on the other hand, all produced both conventional and minicars, and together had roughly 30 percent of the total car market by 1962. These producers reacted with hostility to MITI's proposal, and after a series of unsuccessful discussions, it was dropped.

MITI, it should be noted, did not try to force consolidation upon reluctant car manufacturers. Industry attitudes and the limitations of MITI's direct power kept it from ordering formal combinations of producers.

Development Law for Specific Industries. In 1962 MITI was concerned with structure in several major industries, including motor cars, petrochemicals, and tires. It sought a comprehensive legislative charter to undertake, in cooperation with industry, major programs for producer specialization, establishing appropriate investment levels and promoting mergers and groupings. Toward this end, MITI drafted the Development Law for Specific Industries. The law conferred major financial advantages on the motor car industry and on other industries, if they chose to participate. The programs themselves would be jointly conceived by the manufacturers, the commercial banks, and MITI.

The wide scope of this ambitious proposal attracted attention from many elements of government. The leadership of the ruling Liberal Democratic Party strongly favored enactment. The Fair Trade Commission (FTC) and the car producers themselves generally opposed the legislation. The FTC complained that the law would extend the government's intimacy with industry beyond desirable limits, while the motor car manufacturers did not want to put their autonomy at risk. More importantly, even the secondary producers did not yet feel any financial necessity to seek consolidation. While the industry was exceptionally competitive, it was uniformly profitable during the early 1960s for major producers, all of whom earned a sufficient return on their investment to finance the required growth. Five secondary producers—Toyo Kogyo, Mitsubishi, Fuji, Daihatsu, and Honda—gained or maintained their market share between 1963 and 1965 while following relatively conservative financial policies.

Other Measures. The draft law failed because of the opposition of producers in the motor car and other designated industries. The government, however, did not give up its effort to make mergers financially attractive should the occasion arise. Motor car manufacturers qualified for the existing government Investment and Loan Program, while the Japan Development Bank would help to finance any bona fide formal merger or cooperative production affiliation. In addition, the two ministries devised and secured approval of a special tax deductible allowance which rewarded mergers. It reduced tax liability for a limited period in proportion to the increase in a firm's capital through a merger.

MITI did not limit its techniques of persuasion to the financial area. The ministry was discriminating in its approval of foreign technology introduction by domestic producers. In 1968, for instance, Toyo Kogyo, the third-ranking car producer and a staunch opponent of consolidation, was denied permission to import radiator technology from Renault. Only later, in conjunction with the approval of an application from Nissan to import essentially the same technology, was Toyo's request granted.

By the middle 1960s, MITI's concern with structure was acute. Two facts were clear by 1965. First, the fragmentation of market share was pronounced: eight firms each held at least 5 percent of total vehicle production. Only Toyota and Nissan were internationally viable. Second, the prospect for continued protection from foreign competition was limited. In October 1965, quantitative restrictions on passenger car imports were removed. During the preceding year, Japan had become a member of the Organization for Economic Cooperation and Development (OECD) and had given a commitment to liberalize restrictions on foreign capital investment. To defuse the inevitable liberalization of investment in the motor car industry became MITI's dominant objective for the remainder of the 1960s. Quite apart from the fact that consolidation would strengthen the domestic industry competitively against American capital, merger and affiliation of Japanese producers were the only effective ways to deny foreign manufacturers domestic partners. A marginal, independent domestic car producer would be the naturally desirable partner for foreign companies trying to enter the Japanese market.

Nissan/Prince Merger. The first major consolidation in the industry occurred in 1966 with the merger of Nissan and Prince. Although financial needs prompted the merger, MITI seized the opportunity when it arose and took steps to encourage it. The merger was consummated in May 1966. The negotiations principally involved the two companies and their banks, although the chief executive of the Japan Development Bank also entered the discussions and promised financial assistance to the merger.

The merger served many interests. MITI accomplished its strategic aim—the merger of a secondary producer with one of the two dominant companies. Nissan, which had struggled with inadequate passenger car capacity, acquired Prince's modern and under-utilized plant. Prince's technical staff was highly regarded, and its dealer network gave Nissan improved distribution coverage. Prince, of course, was financially extricated, and the bankruptcy of one of the country's major firms was avoided.

The Japan Development Bank extended roughly $15 million in credit to the merged company. This was the Bank's first loan to the motor car industry since MITI announced the new criteria for loans three years earlier. Only one other government-sponsored loan was made subsequently, when Hino became affiliated with Toyota later in 1966.

Producer Affiliations. The Nissan-Prince merger apparently stimulated other manufacturers to pursue consolidation. Within two years of the merger, six separate car producer affiliation arrangements were negotiated, though only two were consummated. These six were not formal merger proposals but rather "groupings," or limited bilateral arrangements by which minority shares were exchanged, overlapping production was rationalized, parts were standardized, and dealerships were shared. The six negotiations are summarized below:

Year	Companies	Outcome
1966	Toyota-Hino	Success
1966	Fuji-Isuzu	Failure
1967	Toyota-Daihatsu	Success
1967	Mitsubishi-Fuji-Isuzu	Failure
1967	Mitsubishi-Isuzu	Failure
1968	Nissan-Isuzu	Failure

The only successes involve Toyota. In both cases, the product lines were complementary: Hino's trucks and Daihatsu's minicars with Toyota's conventional passenger cars. Both affiliations were arranged by Mitsui Bank, which was the primary creditor for all three firms. At the request of the manufacturers, MITI did not intervene in the discussions.

MITI's effort to bring Nissan and Isuzu together was one of several attempts in the late 1960s to consolidate the industry around Toyota and Nissan. Merger efforts focused on grouping secondary producers around the two dominant ones, but MITI failed to push through these mergers. An effort to merge Nissan and Toyo Kogyo met with similar resistance. Eventually, Nissan and Fuji did merge, but MITI did not play a significant role.

At the end of the decade, it was clear that MITI's attempts to consolidate the industry had failed. Neither the three-group nor the two-group concept had materialized. MITI's legislative programs for consolidation had not been enacted, and its financial incentives for affiliation had drawn limited response. The effect of this failure can be seen in the accelerated flow of foreign capital into the industry after the liberalization of restrictions which occurred in the early 1970s. Isuzu and General Motors joined forces, as did Chrysler and Mitsubishi. Toyo Kogyo and Ford also formed many agreements. On the other hand, it is the indigenous and wholly Japanese producers which continue to dominate the Japanese market. Nissan, Toyota, and Honda have been the most successful companies, and Toyo Kogyo, despite its unsuccessful wankel engine gamble, remains in fourth place.

EXPORT ASSISTANCE. A further way in which the Japanese government has aided the automobile industry is through export assistance, including some financial support and direct functional assistance. Such aid was directed toward the development of overseas marketing and distribution capacity for Japanese car producers.

Financial Support. In 1949, six motor car manufacturers established an Export Promotion Association to perform basic overseas market research. The Ministry of Commerce and Industry subsidized the research and the preparation of catalogues written in English—perhaps Japan's first car export marketing step.

Long-term export credit offered by the Export-Import Bank of Japan dates from 1950. The Bank historically emphasized heavy equipment industries with large export financing requirements, including cars, ships, and locomotives. Its lending was typically supplemented by commercial bank credit, with terms advantageous to the borrower. Since the early 1970s, however, preferential export borrowing terms have been disappearing.

The first tax assistance came in the form of an export income deduction provision in 1953. This system, which provided a maximum deduction of 8 percent of net export income, was initiated by MITI and approved by the Ministry of Finance. Less than 150,000 passenger cars were exported under this tax exemption, and the Japanese discontinued the practice in 1964 in compliance with GATT regulations.

In the same year, a series of more indirect financial incentives was established, including measures that permitted exporting firms to establish tax-free reserves for overseas marketing development and investment. Most notable among these income reserves was that for "overseas market cultivation," which allowed a firm to shield 0.5 percent of its export sales from tax. In addition, an accelerated depreciation schedule tied to export performance was instituted. A manufacturer who increased his export business relative to competitors or to the previous year's performance qualified for special accelerated schedules on export-related capital investment. For the rapidly growing firm these reserve and depreciation measures become a permanent and not insignificant source of funds. Suspension of these special provisions was announced in 1972.

Functional Assistance. Since the early postwar years, the Japanese government has made an effort to improve the quality of the country's exports, requiring that exports of specific products be inspected either by government or by industry association authorities. In addition, since the Export Insurance Law of 1950, government has provided Japanese exporters with default insurance. Through the Heavy Machinery Export Council, manufacturers played an important role in developing the insurance program, insisting on lower premiums and extended coverage. In 1965 Japan's official export promotion agency—Japan External Trade Rehabilitation Organization—established the Chicago Automobile Parts Center to promote Japanese car exports to help solve the logistical problems of the overseas car part business, and to undertake market research. MITI partially subsidized the Auto Parts Center.

Like other forms of government assistance to the industry, however, overseas investment and export assistance declined in the early 1970s and is now virtually nonexistent.

V

ALUMINUM AND SHIPBUILDING INDUSTRIES

Next comes a discussion of two industries in decline—aluminum and shipbuilding.

Industries in serious trouble are not new to Japan. Japan's biggest manufacturing employer, the textile industry, has been in decline for twenty years. It has uncompetitively high wages, too many small and inefficient producers, and no advantage in raw material costs or market access against its Asian competitors. Today the industry employs 300,000 fewer people than in 1965, and the loss has been concentrated in a few regions. Still, the rapid growth of the economy during the late 1960s and early 1970s has absorbed these workers, and serious political repercussions have been avoided. Japan's major capital-intensive industries—steel, aluminum, synthetic textile fibers—have undergone serious recessions in the past, but these were cyclical in nature. Recession cartels and countercyclical monetary and fiscal policy always brought recovery.

In the late 1970s, however, a number of major industries are basically uncompetitive internationally and unlikely ever to recover fully. They include aluminum smelting, chemical fertilizers, ferroalloys, plywood, sugar refining, and synthetic textile fibers, among others. The source of their structural problems varies. Some have uncompetitive energy costs, while others have too high priced raw materials. Some have been poorly managed, while others are simply natural casualties of the industrialization of the Third World. The solution to the serious problems posed by these declining industries has not yet been found. The Structurally Depressed Industries Law enacted in May 1978 was drafted by MITI and passed by the Diet, but consensus has not yet developed to enable it to be used effectively. Major producers have been unwilling either to merge or to trim permanently their operations, and the national political leadership has already, in one notable shipbuilding case, shown itself unwilling to allow an uncompetitive firm to become bankrupt.

The law designates several industries—aluminum smelting and shipbuilding among them—as structurally depressed, and it sets forth criteria to cover others. To be eligible for reconstruction measures, an industry must have severe overcapacity, more than one-half of the firms must be in serious financial difficulty, and two-thirds of the firms must sign a petition seeking designation as a depressed industry. Once designated, the responsible ministry may develop a stabilization plan for the industry wherein the ministry forecasts supply and demand, measures excess capacity, and identifies plants to be closed or cut back. Where scrapping capacity brings real financial stress, the law authorizes a loan guarantee trust fund to encourage private banks to extend further credit to their ailing debtors. Most of this loan guarantee fund is subscribed by the Japan Development Bank and other public banks. To mitigate the employment effects of a reduction in physical capacity, two additional laws were passed in 1978. The first of these provides for an extension of unemployment benefits by ninety days and retraining allowances both for retained and dismissed employees. The second provides a variety of financial relief measures to small and medium-size firms in the depressed regions.

The law is typically Japanese in its intended operation. MITI is obliged to consult with those inside the industry, and labor unions are given an advisory voice. The law empowers MITI to restrict new investment in the industry. The FTC is able to review the stabilization plan to ensure that it is not anti-competitive. Finally, the companies in trouble and MITI have to agree on a workable plan. Despite its good lineage, to date the law has been applied neither to aluminum nor to shipbuilding—two of the most protracted problem industries.

ALUMINUM

Japan has never been a world competitive producer of aluminum. The industry has grown at the same rate as the economy, but the volume of imports of aluminum was two or three times as great as exports in the period 1970 to 1976. Since 1974 the industry has been in especially difficult shape. Electricity is a key cost element in the smelting of aluminum. (About 15,000 kilowatt hours are required to refine one ton.) Since the oil shock in 1973, electricity prices for Japanese aluminum smelters have been about twice those in Europe and about four to five times those in North America. Japan's price for electricity is about 8 to 9 yen per kwh as against 1 to 2 yen in Canada. As a result, Japanese domestic aluminum costs in early 1978 were 320,000 yen per ton (of which one-third is electricity) compared with an import price of about 280,000 yen per ton (c.i.f. price).

In 1977, domestic capacity in the industry was about 1.1 million tons, with production at 650,000 tons; over 500,000 tons were imported. In that year, operating losses in the industry amounted to about 20 billion yen. Results in 1978 were even worse. Two major public policy issues face the industry: How much capacity reduction should occur, and should it be scrapping or mothballing? What should be the rate of allowable imports?

The producers disagree among themselves on these issues, but the firms in the industry would prefer short-term reversible measures, such as a production cartel, rather than permanent capacity reduction. They want a very limited scrapping of capacity (no more than 25 percent), and they claim that Japan cannot afford to let imports supply too large a share of consumption for economic security reasons. Finally, the industry wants to maintain corporate autonomy with no mergers or groupings.

MITI, on the other hand, wants at least a one-third reduction of capacity, with a higher proportion of scrapping than mothballing of facilities. One idea current in MITI today is to combine the current fourteen plants and seven producers into two large groups, with important operating and investment decisions made at the group level. MITI also would like to rely more on imports, which are far lower in cost; it claims that Japanese overseas aluminum projects such as Sumitomo (Indonesia), Nippon Light Metal (Canada), and Mitsui (Brazil) will add about 25 percent to Japanese-owned capacity and will guarantee sources of supply.

MITI and the industry also disagree on the question of rate of import flow. Currently, the volume of imports is about four times that of exports; imports account for about one-third of the total market. Imports come in two ways: via trading companies, which average low price imports with high price-affiliated domestic product to sell to all users, and via independent importers, who do not average and sell low priced imports directly to large users.

One producer wants the government to set up a public company to buy all aluminum, both imported and domestically produced, and sell to users. This step would allow the state to enforce a limit on imports by permitting only captive flows to enter. The producers also want an electricity rate subsidy so that they can supply competitively priced aluminum to the home market.

MITI regards protectionism via a state trading company as politically unacceptable inside and outside Japan; in any event it would not solve the industry's cost problems. The electricity subsidy is ruled out as being too costly, given the differential between Japanese rates and the rates of Canada, Norway, and other producing countries. MITI proposed instead the use of a tariff quota device whereby duty would be cut on a specified import volume but the user price would stay the same. The difference would go to a restructuring loan fund for the industry. MITI has estimated that about 3 billion yen could be available from this fund in the first year.

Thus MITI and the industry are at an impasse. A committee consisting of independent mediators is searching for appropriate means of rationalizing the industry, but so far has not succeeded. Although the law has been in effect for a year, still no solution is in sight. MITI is essentially market-conscious and is looking for a permanent structure solution, resisting protection and agreeing to subsidize only when there is some rationalization. The companies do not want to surrender their autonomy, or to regroup or cut a significant amount of capacity permanently. The stronger companies seem willing to wait for a survival-of-the-fittest solution, and many of the companies in the industry are part of larger multi-business companies which can absorb financial losses for a while, enabling them to resist pressures.

SHIPBUILDING

The shipbuilding industry provides an example of an industry that has gone through all three phases of development in Japan. In the 1950s and early 1960s, shipbuilding was a priority industry that received substantial government assistance in its attempt to gain international competitive dominance. In the late 1960s and early 1970s, the industry became a world leader, and government involvement in the industry waned. Now, in the late 1970s, the industry is declining with the rise of new developing country competitors (hastened by the collapse of the tanker market over the past few years).

The history of the industry reflects the full cycle of Japanese industrial policy. Shipbuilding was covered in the initial machinery reconstruction acts passed in 1956, and companies received considerable aid in modernizing capital equipment. The government gave shipbuilding priority because of the need for a strong shipping industry in an island nation like Japan and because steel and labor are the major costs of ship construction. In the 1950s Japan had an abundance of low cost labor, and steel was an investment priority.

Shipbuilding developed through Zaibatsu around sister trading companies and shipping companies. Some of the steel mills also formed their own shipbuilding companies. Thus the industry included a significant number of large powerful companies. Because of the steel and labor advantages, a number of smaller companies also grew up during the 1960s; these companies tended to specialize around particular types of ships.

During the initial phase of industry development, the Ministry of Transport (which has no jurisdiction over the industry) and the Ministry of Finance used various means to assist the introduction of new technology and also to encourage rationalization. The government formed an industry development association to share techniques and to assist in overseas marketing. A key factor in the development of export markets in this period was the use of sugar import measures (described in Chapter VI) to allow Japanese shipbuilders to supply ships for export below their costs: shipbuilders received a compensating subsidy in the form of lucrative profits from the licensed import of raw sugar.

In 1959 an advisory council on shipbuilding and shipping was established. It authorized interest rate subsidies on loans to the shipbuilding industry for approved mergers, an interest rate subsidy to shipping companies in Japan to buy Japanese ships, and a series of favorable tax measures. The Japan Development Bank (JDB) was instrumental in providing loans to the industry, and a number of the quasi-public and private banks were also encouraged to participate. In the early stages about 70 percent of all industry financing was from the JDB. In some cases the interest rate subsidy went as far as a deferral of repayment up to fifteen years.

The government provided significant tax benefits to the industry. It allowed reserves for price fluctuations to be tax free, a large special depreciation account, establishment of export and investment losses reserves to avoid taxes, and tax and other financial incentives for investment in overseas market development. In one company studied, about 5 billion yen per year—one-third of its tax burden—was subsidized through these tax measures alone during the mid-1960s.

While low interest and deferred loans for consolidation, price subsidies through the sugar license, and tax subsidies aided the industry's development, perhaps the most significant assistance to shipbuilding came from customer financing provided at very favorable terms through the Japanese Export-Import Bank. During the 1960s, about 70-80 percent of all loans made by the Bank were in the shipbuilding industry, and the terms of some of these loans provided a considerable subsidy to the manufacturers. Both the easy availability of financing and the competitive rates were of great assistance as Japan expanded its world market share.

By the late 1960s, Japan was the world's lowest cost producer of ships. The provision of low cost steel from Japan's efficient steel industry, the relatively cheap price of Japanese labor (pre-yen revaluations), and the large scale of Japanese shipyards allowed by the rapid growth of the industry during its development phases—all contributed to Japan's dominance in world shipbuilding. In the early and mid-1970s, Japan launched over 50 percent of all the world's ships, and shipbuilding companies were highly profitable.

During the maturity phase (late 1960s, early 1970s), government assistance to the industry all but disappeared. The government reduced tax subsidies, eliminated export price subsidies, virtually ended the JDB loans by refusing to allow deferrals on payments, and reduced export-import financing considerably. During the early 1970s, for example, one company which had received a 32 percent reduction in taxes during the growth phase (mid-1960s) received only a 9 percent tax reduction (entirely from depreciation); it did not receive any JDB loans.

The Japanese industry entered its declining phase after the 1973-74 tanker boom. In 1975 Japan launched 17 million gross tons of ships; in 1978 its launchings had fallen to 6.3 million tons. The collapse of the tanker market was the major cause of this decline, but Japan's market share also dropped (from 49.7 percent in 1975 to 34.7 percent in 1978) as lower wage countries like Korea, Spain, Brazil, and Taiwan increased their share. There was a rise in Japan's share of the market in 1979, but it is still significantly below mid-1970s levels. Currently, about 150,000 people are employed in shipbuilding in Japan, of which about half are considered redundant. As a result of the market collapse, twenty-eight small and medium-sized shipbuilders went into bankruptcy between March 1977 and March 1978. Most of the large companies have withstood the serious situation so far because they are associated with major Zaibatsu or steel companies and can absorb losses.

The Ministry of Transport established an advisory commission for the shipbuilding industry which in 1976 recommended significant cutbacks in the industry's capacity in order to achieve a supply-demand balance by 1985. The ministry has proposed that the seven major companies reduce capacity by about 40 percent, and the government wants small companies to close down. A plan to boost demand by retiring government ships ahead of schedule and expanding Japanese exports of ships to developing countries as a form of economic assistance has also been put forward. Finally, the government wants to refocus some industry capacity on liquid natural gas tankers, floating factories, and other, more sophisticated types of ships.

The Structurally Depressed Industries Law has given the Ministry of Transport tools to realize these objectives. However, the firms in the industry cannot agree among themselves or with the government on a plan to bring about this rationalization. Large and small firms have disagreed about who should bear the burden of capacity reductions. Finally, the industry does not want to scrap capacity permanently, and is calling for greater temporary financial assistance from the government. In January, interest rate subsidies to the shipping companies were restored, and there are some signs that the government will provide some temporary subsidies even without the completion of a rationalization plan: the employment and bankruptcy developments in shipbuilding have increased political pressures to rescue the industry.

The Sasebo case illustrates these pressures.[1] Sasebo Heavy Industries is the eighth largest shipbuilder in Japan. Its major stockholders are Nippon Steel and Nippon Kokan, Japan's two largest steel companies, and its major bank is Dai Ichi Kanqyo. It is a major employer in the city of Sasebo, so its announcement in early 1978 of financial difficulty and its intention to seek voluntary early retirement by one thousand employees produced concern. Concern later became crisis when the major stockholders decided not to guarantee future loans, and the banks refused additional funds without guarantees. Confidence in the company's management was low and could not be restored. The major ministries involved—Finance and Transport—and the Bank of Japan chose not to arrange a rescue, and were prepared to see the company declare bankruptcy. The consensus of the regular policymaking apparatus was that the company should be allowed to fail.

This became politically unacceptable, however, when the work force and the Sasebo community petitioned members of the Diet, including the Prime Minister, to intervene. The Prime Minister

[1]This discussion draws heavily on an unpublished paper by Kent E. Caldor of Harvard University entitled "The Emerging Politics of Aid for the Uncompetitive: The Case of Sasebo Heavy Industries."

requested the two ministries to find a solution. It was not forthcoming. Then the Prime Minister *ordered* that a solution be found. Eventually the banks, major stockholders, and ministries put together a package which the banks grudgingly accepted. It included some government financial relief, a hastily arranged American ship repair business to bolster demand, a syndicated bank loan from eighteen different banks, and a modest new capital infusion from the major shareholders. All of this was premised on a carefully negotiated change of management.

The Sasebo case is interesting primarily as a demonstration that politics can (and occasionally will) thwart the regular policy consensus process. The policymaking community had reached a clear consensus—Sasebo should be permitted to fail—but the nation's highest elected officials (members of the Diet) could not resist expedient measures, and they overrode standard procedures. The ministries were aggrieved at this outcome because it clearly complicated the solution of the broader shipbuilding problem. Shipbuilders' resistance to the "rational" schemes of the public policy community has grown.

The resolution of the shipbuilding crisis is still unclear. Some of the major companies have been able to shift their capacity to other businesses, such as heavy industrial machinery and plant exports. The underlying obstacle to consensus is less whether the problem will go away and more how should the cutbacks be distributed among the producers. The producers are a heterogeneous lot—small versus large, diversified versus specialized—and they have very different reactions to any proposed solution. Recently a company was formed to purchase excess stocks. Loans totalling 90 billion yen have been obtained—90 percent from private financial institutions, 5 percent from shipbuilding companies, and 5 percent from government. The government has played the role of catalyst in this venture.

SUMMARY

The plight of the aluminum and shipbuilding industries in the late 1970s in Japan is instructive. Traditionally Japan has demonstrated an ability to face major issues squarely. The Structurally Depressed Industries Law, by attempting to cushion the social problems at the same time that it accelerates the restructuring of industry, is in this tradition. So far the law has not been successfully implemented owing to disagreements among the parties which must reach consensus. In addition, political concerns have intervened. The challenge to develop a long-term sound public policy is great.

VI

INDUSTRIAL MACHINERY AND INFORMATION ELECTRONICS INDUSTRY

The last two case studies to be examined focus on sectors which are growing rapidly and are of increasing importance to Japan's future international competitive position: industrial machinery and information electronics. These studies show how industrial policy in Japan is applied to businesses where there is significant technology change and where Western companies are still competitively formidable. Both these industries are undergoing changes in their competitive structure, and the challenge to industrial policy has been to anticipate and to lead events in the marketplace.

In industrial machinery, the areas of intense competition and high growth have shifted away from single machine manufacture toward developing computer-controlled production systems and supplying whole plants, particularly for the rapid growth export market. Accordingly, government policy has focused less on industrial concentration and more on systems research and development and export financing.

In the information electronics sector, which includes data processing, telecommunications, and other applications of semi-conductor technology, competition among the major international companies and economies is intensive, and the Japanese government has made an enormous commitment to advancing the Japanese position. A complex pattern of government-sponsored cooperation in both research and development and equipment leasing has for at least a decade accompanied the intense competition among Japanese companies in designing, manufacturing, and marketing their own systems. Government has sought the advantages of both large, central research efforts at a national level and unrestrained competition for market share of a large and growing domestic market among the companies. While the government and the industry often disagree and the results of some programs have been disappointing, it is clear that Japan's global position has advanced materially and that the government financing and coordination have been crucial to this progress.

JAPANESE INDUSTRIAL POLICY

INDUSTRIAL MACHINERY

The Japanese have long regarded the machinery industry as critically important to their country's development. A knowledge-intensive industry employing highly skilled labor, it has a high growth potential and is shielded from competition from developing countries. Japan currently accounts for less than 11 percent of all OECD industrial machinery exports—behind Germany, the United States, and the United Kingdom, and only slightly ahead of France. This industry is destined for aggressive development in the future. Industrial policy for this industry has evolved in response to changes in the competitive position of machinery businesses throughout the world, and the aim of the industrial policy is for Japan to progress toward leadership in the industry.

THE CHANGING COMPETITIVE POSITION

In the 1950s and 1960s, the machinery industry consisted of two basic types of businesses. The first was the production of mechanical components such as gears, bearings, valves, heat exchangers, springs, etc. Production of mechanical components usually consists of pressing, machining, and some type of finishing operation. Competitive success depends primarily on large-scale production and long runs of standard products together with a sufficient volume of production to be able to dedicate production lines for special products. Marketing and engineering, while important, tend to be less significant, and large volume production enables an easier amortization of costs.

The second basic type of business was machine assembly, in which mechanical components and structural metals and castings are assembled into paper machines, steel rolling mills, metalworking machine tools, etc. Since machine redesigns have an enormous effect on sales, research and development is crucial in this type of business. It has traditionally required coupling prime mover technology and metallurgical engineering to produce faster, more accurate, more powerful machines. The scale of production is less important to competitive success, although in some cases, large scale may enable a producer to gain advantage by manufacturing components within his own organization.

Two broad industry trends have had a significant impact on industrial machinery businesses in the 1970s. The first is the development of so-called "systems businesses," or the sale of whole plants. Various machines are assembled with construction materials into whole plants and are sold and installed as a package by one producer (though he may subcontract parts of it).

One reason for the growth of systems businesses has been the increasing importance of developing countries as markets for machines. As industrialization proceeds in OPEC and Comecon and advanced developing countries, non-OECD countries have come to account for roughly one half of all OECD machinery purchases. These countries are less able to design their own plants, whether for ethylene production or food processing, and prefer to buy them ready-made. The ability to sell, for example, a dairy separator may therefore hinge on the ability to offer the whole plant in which it will operate.

The growth of systems businesses has also been accelerated by progress in process control. Coordinated systems now allow the computer-centralized (or microprocessor-distributed) control of a whole factory, increasing the effectiveness of industrial machines. Maximum efficiency in the overall process is achieved by designing an entire plant for a given application rather than by assembling well-designed individual machines.

The development of the whole plant sale businesses has increased the significance of applications engineering in the overall cost structure of the industry. Because purchases are bigger, the importance of long-term buyer financing and insurance of seller's risk has also increased.

The other major development in the machinery industry in the 1970s has been the introduction of new technologies to be integrated into machinery design, particularly miniature electronics, lasers, and ultrasonics. Intelligent control in machines, the use of laser cutting and printing, and ultrasonic testing are examples. As a result, machinery makers have had to undertake massive research and development in unfamiliar fields in order to remain competitive in the industry.

JAPAN'S PLACE IN THE WORLD INDUSTRY

Japan was far behind major European and U.S. companies in production and design capability in the 1950s and early 1960s partly because of war damage, but by the mid-1970s had virtually closed the gap. As its producers have become more successful, the Japanese government has shifted its policy from massive aid and very close direction to a looser form of assistance and cooperation. The types of aid offered have also changed along with the needs of the industry, as it evolved from one which imported technology to one on the cutting edge of new developments.

Japanese government policy has recognized the complexity of the machinery industry, which is made up of both small and large companies with very different cost structures. Because of this heterogeneity, Japanese policy toward industrial machinery has consisted of almost one hundred programs over the past twenty-five years. We will mention only a few important ones.

Active policy in the industry began in 1956 with the Extraordinary Measures Law for the Rehabilitation of the Machinery Industry, aimed at rationalizing the industry's production and creating initial demand for its products.[1] The law focused on basic components and some simple machinery. Twenty-one industry areas were eventually designated under the law, including bearings, springs, gears, simple presses, castings, and machine tools.

Between 1956 and 1960, the Japan Development Bank provided funds for modernization of equipment; MITI authorized rationalization cartels for purchasing parts and importing materials; standards were set for the industry, and guidelines were established for production technology improvement. During this period the government provided almost four hundred loans totalling about 10 billion yen. Roughly 25 percent went to the machine tools industry, 13 percent to car parts, and the rest to various component makers of tools and gears. The main goal at this stage was to impose basic standards on an industry made up of thousands of small producers. To the extent that these standards could not be met by weaker companies and they left the industry, the industry as a whole was rationalized. In general, however, rationalization measures were carried out primarily within individual firms.

In 1961 the Extraordinary Measures Law was extended and aimed at further rationalization, this time through merger and joint investment rather than within one company. The government made available Japan Development Bank loans and preferential tax rates to encourage joint investments and mergers, and the Small Business Finance Corporation (established in the late 1950s) began to make loans to firms in the industry to assist rationalization. Between 1961

[1]Before 1956, the Reconversion Finance Bank and the Japan Development Bank had helped to rebuild some of the large machinery manufacturers from before the war in order to supply the needs of UN forces in the Korean conflict. This aid, however, was not part of any industrial plan.

and 1965, the JDB made loans totalling over 34 billion yen on more than 644 projects, primarily in the car parts, machine tools, and bearings industries.

Throughout this period, there was a twofold policy approach appropriate to the machinery industry. In areas like car parts and bearings, where large-scale production and long runs are essential to achieve low cost, mergers were encouraged. In other areas, like the making of special springs, gears, or castings, or certain parts of the machine tool industry, where scale of production is less important, modernization was encouraged within the small companies. Industry associations were formed to facilitate the flow of information, and rationalization cartels were authorized, but the emphasis was on financing (through the Small Business Finance Corporation) to modernize equipment.

By the mid-1960s, these measures had succeeded in rationalizing the simple machine industry. When the law was extended again, emphasis shifted to making the companies internationally competitive. Major overseas enterprises were carefully examined as to size, capacity, and level of technology. In order to improve the structure of the Japanese industry, a cartel was formed to allocate product categories among companies and group enterprises and to establish joint ventures. In some businesses, like chemical machinery, individual producers were encouraged to cooperate in the development of new products; in other businesses, like machine tools, certain enterprises were encouraged to drop certain products. In other cases, such as printing machinery, joint ventures and mergers were sponsored. The JDB provided over 30 billion yen during the period 1965-69 for this purpose.

In general, the industrial policy of the late 1950s was aimed at improving individual company efficiency; in the early 1960s, basic mergers to consolidate the industry were encouraged; and in the late 1960s, emphasis shifted to the encouragement of greater specialization.

PROTECTION AND STIMULATION OF THE HOME MARKET

Throughout the 1950s and early 1960s, only machinery which could not be made in Japan was allowed to be imported. This guaranteed a market for Japanese producers and encouraged foreign producers to license their technology or to form joint ventures in Japan, since outright exports to Japan were impossible.

In addition, a series of loan programs helped domestic machinery suppliers become more competitive in the home market (Table VI.1). In addition to these loan programs, a series of special depreciation laws were enacted both to promote mechanization and to encourage the purchase of Japanese-made machinery. (A recent survey by the Japanese taxation agency reports that between 1963 and 1976 the government forfeited over 174 billion yen of tax revenue in these special depreciation programs.) Finally, in 1961, the government instituted a credit insurance system designed to protect the suppliers of machinery against defaults by customers, particularly small enterprises.

Table VI.1

LOAN PROGRAM EXAMPLES

Between 1964 and 1969, a program existed to allow Japanese producers to compete against foreign companies with installment low interest sales.[a] The Industrial Bank of Japan and the Long Term Credit Bank provided funds to enable the domestic industry to offer similar credit conditions to domestic users of machinery. The funds came from the Treasury. Loans were provided in the area of machine tools, plastic moulding machinery, printing machinery, etc. Loans of more than 25 billion yen were made during this period.

In 1974 the Japan Development Bank lent roughly 3 billion yen to manufacturers of packaging machinery, allowing them to establish a joint venture leasing company specializing in packaging machinery.

A series of measures during the 1960s and 1970s to assist leasing of labor-saving, safe new machinery (including packaging machinery, metalworking machine tools, conveying equipment, etc.) was provided by the Long Term Credit Bank, Industrial Bank of Japan, and Nippon Credit from Treasury financing.

Japan Development Bank made loans in the 1960s to enable manufacturing companies to introduce new machinery in a comprehensive way so that the whole production process could be modernized.

[a]This is a method of selling which provides long-term low interest credit to the buyer. The ownership of the equipment is transferred at the time of sale to leasing companies.

These programs served two purposes: they encouraged the modernization of all Japanese industry, and at the same time they aided the Japanese machinery industry.

EXPORT PROMOTION

The Japanese developed a variety of highly incentive means to encourage exports of machinery, including the formation of associations, export price subsidies of various sorts, both short- and long-term export financing, and tax incentives.

The Japan Machinery Exporters Association was established in 1953 with a subsidy from the government to provide advice on technology together with information and promotional services to assist Japanese exports. The association is exempt from the anti-monopoly laws and can help the industry to implement orderly marketing agreements, to put price floors under exports, and to negotiate with MITI on export matters. With six hundred members, it can coordinate the formation of groups of companies to handle large overseas plant export orders. It is also in a position to coordinate financing arrangements and to provide government contacts in foreign countries.

In the early 1950s, a "linking" system enabled Japanese exporters of machinery to price competitively on international markets. The government controlled the import of raw sugar, but in order to provide a subsidy to machinery exporters, the control of raw sugar imports was handed over to the Machinery Exporters Association. The association sold the sugar at the international price, and the profit they obtained was used to compensate machinery exporters who had incurred losses in building export sales by pricing at international or even lower levels. This "linking" system was extremely important in shipbuilding as well.

Partly in order to improve its position in international trade negotiations, Japan has sinced reduced direct export grants to a minimal level. The only major grant program still operative is the assistance given to the export associations by the bicycle racing fund, which totals about 3 to 4 billion yen per year. Loans, on the other hand, remain a major factor in export promotion. The Japan Export-Import Bank is much like those in other countries in its operations, and an ever-increasing proportion of its funds has gone to the machinery industry. Both supplier and buyer credits are extended according to rules laid down by the OECD.

In all of these loan programs, MITI has review rights which give them influence over individual companies. Any transaction by the Export-Import Bank not settled within six months must be submitted to MITI for approval. Thus while MITI does not actively screen each transaction, it has a means of review whenever it is necessary. In Japan, the controls on foreign transactions have not been dismantled, just relaxed. Similarly, reviews are made of the credit worthiness of all manufacturers and exporters. This evaluation was especially important in the 1950s and 1960s, when capital was short and the export advance bills given by the bank were crucial to overall company financing. This made exports very popular, especially with smaller machinery companies.

Tax incentives have also played an important role in export production. The government has used a variety of different measures over the years, as shown in Table VI.2.

These measures played a very significant role in the 1960s, but have become less significant in the 1970s. Although several are still technically in effect, only the technology export income deduction is significant today. In 1976 these measures in total added about 32 billion yen to the cash flow of companies of which almost 20 billion came from the technology provision in the machinery industry. This accounted for about 5 percent of taxes actually paid in the industry. In addition to these measures, the government has two export insurance programs--one covering all industries and another compensating for losses caused by inadequate consultation on overseas machinery projects.

POLICY IN THE 1970s AND 1980s

By 1970 the process of industry rationalization had essentially been completed. World-scale component producers coexisted in Japan with a number of efficient producers of machines. The Japanese industry enjoyed a predominance in its home market and had made inroads into world markets for some products, particularly simple machine tools and textile machinery.

In the early 1970s, government policy turned away from rationalization, home market protection and stimulation, and export assistance measures, and toward research and development assistance to companies for whole plant sales abroad. The goals are to move Japan into the forefront of machinery technology, to build world market share by attacking the new growth markets in developing countries, and to build upon strong Japanese process industries to emphasize whole plant sales.

These efforts to guide industry development have achieved considerable success. Japan has only a small export share in ordinary machine tools, compared to Germany and the United States, but a

Table VI.2

EXPORT PROMOTING TAX MEASURES

Years	Measure
1953-1964	Export income deduction *Export income was directly shielded from taxation.*
1953-1959	Export loss reserve system *A reserve against the possibility of cancelled export contracts was non-taxable.*
1953-1959	Special depreciation for overseas offices of trading companies *All depreciable assets in a new office overseas were subject to a 50 percent write-off the first year.*
1959 to present	Technology export income deduction *Companies are allowed to deduct a portion of royalties paid from abroad from their taxable income. The objective is to stimulate saleable technology development.*
1964-1972	Overseas market development reserve *A small portion of the revenue from current exports can be put into reserves from taxable income. Like all Japanese reserves, this must later be returned to the income stream. This provision still applies for small businesses.*
1964 to present	Overseas investment loss reserve *A small percentage of current foreign investment expenditure each year can be put into reserve to insure against investment losses. This reserve fund is non-taxable.*
1964-1972	Export accelerated depreciation *Accelerated depreciation was allowed on capital investment where the output was to be exported. The degree of acceleration depended on the proportion of plant and equipment devoted to export.*
1968-1978	Export special depreciation *An overlay acceleration on the previous provision.*
Early 1950s to present	Free trade zone investment loss reserve *Variation on the overseas investment loss reserve extended for free trade zones.*

high share in numerically controlled machine tools. Over 50 percent of Japan's machinery exports went to non-OECD countries in 1974-76, compared to 40 percent for the United States and 30 percent for Germany. Finally, Japan's most rapid export growth has been in steel mills, chemical plants, and other "whole plant" sales.

Research and Development. The primary thrust of Japanese industrial policy in machinery is currently in research and development. The policy includes grants, loans, and tax subsidies.

A number of grant programs currently operate to benefit industrial machinery businesses. MITI's Agency for Industrial Science and Technology (AIST) administers the government's conventional research and development grants. This program gives matching grants to specific research and development projects proposed by individual companies. On average, about 4 billion yen was provided annually to the industrial machinery sector during 1973-76 and 3 billion during 1977 and 1978. These appropriations have been primarily directed to the area of machine and whole plant integration.

A second source of research and development grants is the national Large-Scale Research project (referred to in Chapter III), which combines resources from the government and companies to fund development in areas of nationally critical technologies. In the industrial machinery area, a seven-year program to develop an ultra-high performance laser-applied complex control system (a highly automated machine tool system) will receive 12 billion yen in government assistance plus individual contributions from companies.

A third source of research and development funding is the Bicycle Rehabilitation Association (JBRA). In 1976 the JBRA awarded almost 5 billion yen for research and development in the machinery area. An additional 150 million yen is awarded from a minicar racing fund. MITI undoubtedly influences, although it does not officially control, these allocations.

Another minor source of government funding is the subsidy for research and development by small businesses. This is administered in matching funds programs primarily through the Subsidies for Important Technologies budget. About 450 million yen was allocated to industrial machinery through this channel in 1976.

Finally, the AIST maintains permanent research laboratories whose work principally benefits the industrial machinery area. These laboratories include the Mechanical Engineering Laboratory in Tokyo and the Industrial Research Institutes in Osaka (materials) and Nagoya (forming processes). About 6 billion yen in financing for these laboratories was provided by AIST in 1976.

In total, between 8 and 10 billion yen per year is spent in direct grants for research and development in the industrial machinery industries in Japan. In addition, there is a complex series of loan programs to stimulate research and development. Over the years this lending, primarily carried on by the Japan Development Bank, has grown steadily and is now well over 30 billion yen per year, of which about 8 to 9 billion on average goes to industrial machinery companies. These project-related loans are essentially a means of providing low cost funds to manufacturers and buyers in areas such as the development of heavy machinery, commercialization of new technologies in industry, development of prototypes for commercial production, and commercialization of new technology for small enterprises. For example, the JDB will finance users' purchase of prototype machinery, manufacturers' purchases of equipment to be used in making new types of machines, and the actual development of new types of machines.

The final series of measures the government uses to aid technology development involves tax incentives for research and development. Twenty-five percent of all new spending on research and development can be taken by a company as a direct credit; these credits were worth about 12 billion yen to the machinery industry in 1976. In addition, the government allows special depreciation on equipment. Although the impact of this provision is hard to measure, we estimate its annual value at roughly 5 billion yen.

From 1968 until 1975, a special depreciation program existed for machinery embodying commercial application of new technologies. Regional property taxes as well as corporate income taxes were shielded by this program, which assisted both users of new machinery and manufacturers. Overall, about 78 billion yen of equipment was covered in this program during its existence.

Finally, tax credits are allowed on the dues for establishing cooperative research associations among companies. Over twenty-five of these associations have been created, and the funds paid into them can be subtracted from the individual company's income as depreciation. Over the past few years, grants and loans have accounted for 10 to 15 percent of all research and development spending in the machinery industry. Tax credits related to research and development have averaged about 3 percent of the industry's total tax paid.

Whole Plant Sales. A second major thrust of current industrial policy in machinery is to aid whole plant sales. Many of Japan's institutions work effectively together to promote whole plant sales. MITI has published a 400-page book on whole plant selling and has informally assisted the formation of groups of companies to study particular market opportunities. The industry association and trading companies also play an important role in coordination. The informal connections among MITI, the banks, the industry associations, and the companies, along with the legislation which enables cartels to be formed, allow a flexible model of interaction very helpful in making the complex arrangements needed for whole plant sales.

Financing is crucial to the purchase of a large plant, particularly in developing countries, which now account for about half of the market for machinery. Fully 60 percent of Export-Import Bank loans are now directed to plant export; these loans are often supplemented by financing arranged through large banks (to which the government has close ties). The most significant form of financing assistance, however, is government-to-government credit (in yen), often indirectly tied to machinery sales.

Large national projects sold to the governments of other countries can be financed by mechanisms which fall under the broad heading of economic aid, and thus (in contrast to Export-Import Bank loans) are not regulated by the OECD. In Japan, the agency responsible is the Overseas Economic Cooperation Fund, a public policy company funded via the FILP and under the direction of the Ministry of Finance, the Ministry of Foreign Affairs, and the Economic Planning Agency. Yen credits are a highly desirable form of financing from the borrower's point of view: very low interest is charged (3 percent and less); amounts can exceed the value of the narrowly defined project; and longer repayment terms than those of Export-Import or private financing can be provided.

It is often difficult to discover an explicit link between a government-to-government or even a central bank-to-central bank financing package and a particular large machinery or plant order. Yet clearly such connections are there. Though the Japanese feel that the French are the masters at this type of activity, they themselves have devised a number of inventive financing measures, helped by the strength of the yen and Japan's large dollar balances. Apart from sales arranged between governments, the trading companies play the most significant role in arranging financing, making three-cornered deals, and putting together packages for a sale as well as doing promotion and research, etc. The government may review prices or give guidance on selection of a particular subcontractor, but most of the work is done by the manufacturers and trading companies involved.

SUMMARY

Although Japan is currently behind some other OECD countries in the export of industrial machinery, the priority being placed on this industry will clearly make Japan an increasingly formidable competitor. The groundwork being laid by government research and development, whole plant export coordination, and financing programs will no doubt assist the industry greatly over the coming decade. Though these programs have existed for a number of years, their results will be most pronounced in the near future. These measures reinforce the extremely good cooperation among Japanese companies, which allows a prompt and well coordinated response to market opportunities. Western companies in this industry would be well advised to keep a close watch on current and potential Japanese competitors.

INFORMATION ELECTRONICS

Computers and semiconductors are the heart of information electronics. The Japanese government is committed to developing an internationally strong position in computers, and has given the industry significant support. The task of overcoming American leadership is a large one. U.S. companies have over one-third of the Japanese market, dominate their own large domestic market, and are keenly fighting the Japanese challenge. Japan's overall trade balance in computers, including peripherals and attachments, is distinctly negative. In 1977 the value of imports was three times as great as the value of exports, but exports were growing considerably faster. The two leading Japanese producers—Fujitsu and Hitachi—together have had a smaller share of the Japanese market over the last five years than IBM in the value of computers sold or leased. Japanese producers have advanced quickly, but so have manufacturers in other countries.

Most of the Japanese industry is concentrated in six companies—Fujitsu, Hitachi, Nippon Electric, Toshiba, Mitsubishi Electric, and Oki. They all produce computers, peripherals, and semiconductors, and most of them produce telecommunications equipment as well. Jurisdiction over this sector lies primarily with MITI, although the Ministry of Post and Telecommunications has some responsibility for the development of the telecommunications industry.

COMPUTERS

The government's assistance to computers can be reviewed under three categories: technology development, leasing and financing, and market protection.

Technology Development. The government provides funds for approximately one quarter of all computer-related research and development in Japan, while three quarters is funded by the manufacturers of computers and private laboratories. Total computer research and development in Japan in 1976 was 116.5 billion yen. Government grants to companies and associations were 18.9 billion yen. (Major undertakings like the Very Large Scale Integration [VLSI] circuit development project typically involve matching funds from business and government to ensure a worthwhile effort.) Another 5.8 billion yen of public funds was spent in university and government laboratories. In addition to direct government spending, two tax mechanisms—the research and development tax credit and accelerated depreciation of research and development facilities—offer significant assistance to the industry. One estimate puts tax saved by the computer manufacturers at 3.4 billion yen per year, roughly 5 percent of total expenditure on research and development in the industry.

The government has also offered special help to the software sector. In 1967 the Japan Information Processing Development Center was established as a joint venture of government, the major manufacturers, and the software houses to develop general purpose end user application software. The government invested one billion yen in equity and between 1970 and 1977 contributed 8 billion yen in research and development funds. Not surprisingly, Japan Development Bank is the largest lender. Special tax benefits have been made available to the software industry as well.

The principal rationale for government research and development assistance is the small scale of Japanese producers relative to the American leaders—despite the concentration of all major computer and semiconductor activity within a few Japanese firms. Up to the mid-1970s, research and development funded by Fujitsu, Hitachi, and Nippon Electric combined was less than half of IBM's total expenditure on research and development, while the combined semiconductor research and development expenditure of these Japanese companies is less than Texas Instruments' total.

As with other Japanese industries, MITI has tried to use government funds to rationalize the industry's research and development effort. MITI has also tried unsuccessfully to rationalize the industry itself through mergers. The companies have preferred to remain independent, and a system has emerged in which there is cooperation in the funding of new technology projects, rationalization, and concurrent specialization in peripherals, but continued fierce competition in existing products and in the production and marketing of new products.

The first cooperative research and development project was in 1962, when MITI formed an association of Fujitsu, Nippon, and Oki to develop a new computer. After IBM introduced the 360 model in 1964, MITI conceived a more ambitious large-scale computer project and budgeted for 10 billion yen of government funding. In designing this project, MITI matched the five participating companies and tasks very carefully. Fujitsu, Hitachi, and Nippon were asked to build the memory and central processing unit and to develop the operating system software. Toshiba and Oki were asked to build time-sharing peripheral equipment. (Mitsubishi, the sixth competitor, did not join the project.) Later, MITI organized a peripheral equipment production cartel which enabled the six producers (each of whom had low production scale because of substantial product line overlap) to pool and specialize some equipment. The products handled through the cartel included standard peripherals whose design had stabilized and where further innovation was remote. Seven types of punched card and paper tape equipment were cartelized in 1969. Line printers and magnetic drums were added a year later.

In the early 1970s, MITI tried to organize the industry into three groups (Fujitsu/Hitachi, Nippon/Toshiba, and Mitsubishi/Oki), again to force a specialization of development efforts and, it was hoped, a long-term competitive segmentation of the business. Then the target was the IBM 370 series, and a government-sponsored joint development program was conceived. By 1975, however, the targets of this program were obsolete, and an extraordinary joint effort—the VLSI semiconductor project—was substituted. The four-year project involves all major Japanese producers and two government electronics research laboratories in diverse roles; it is budgeted at 72 billion yen. Roughly 40 percent is government-funded. The technical targets are highly ambitious, aimed at developing the "state-of-the-art" technology in both logic and memory circuits. Completion is scheduled for 1980-86. The project's key members are shown in Figure VI.1.

Figure VI.1

VERY LARGE-SCALE INTEGRATION PROJECT

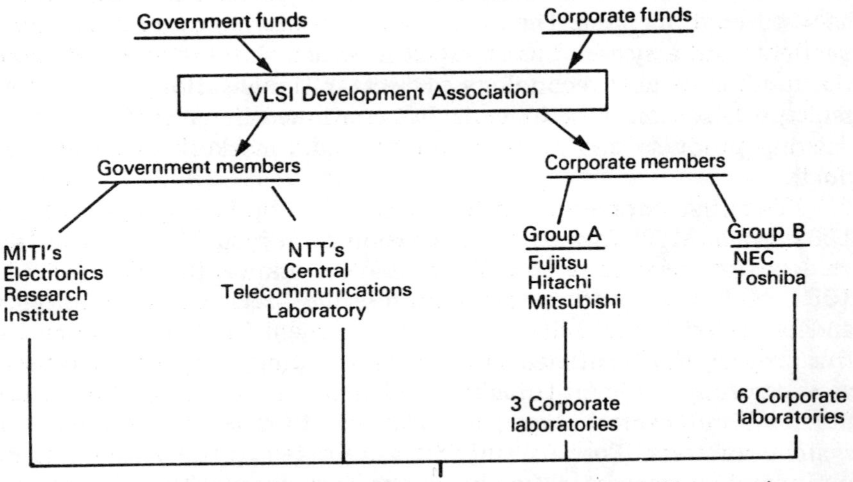

Central Laboratory at MITI's Institute (in close co-operation with respective supporting laboratories)

While Japanese producers have cooperated in these development efforts and benefited enormously, they continue to compete independently on existing products and new systems. MITI has tried to consolidate their computer operations but has failed, and must now rely on the market mechanism to restructure the industry. The business moves extremely fast, and it is not clear whether MITI's policy initiatives of the 1970s to reduce the number of competitors were appropriate. On the one hand, computers will turn out to have been an expensive adventure for some Japanese producers, as for some large American and European companies. On the other hand, it is difficult to predict which company will succeed and in what sector in this rapidly changing business.

Leasing and Financing. Apart from support for research and development, the government's major contribution to the industry has been in giving financial assistance to purchasers of computers—a crucial element in computer marketing.

In the early 1960s, it became clear that by leasing rather than selling computers, IBM was using its financial position to take advantage of its Japanese competitors, who could not compete in the leasing arrangements, though MITI proposed a joint venture of government and computer manufacturers; this joint company would lease only Japanese made computers. Neither the manufacturers nor the Ministry of Finance would accept government equity participation, and the compromise reached in 1961 was a joint venture, with the equity shared among the seven manufacturers then active, financed heavily by the Japan Development Bank. This venture was called the Japan Electronic Computer Corporation (JECC).

JECC purchases computers from the manufacturers and then leases them to customers. At the end of 1978, the gross value of JECC's rented assets was over 400 billion yen. Over one third is financed by the JDB at interest rates roughly one percent below the market rate, while city banks finance most of the rest. JECC has been generally successful, particularly in financing the explosive market growth which took place in the 1960s. In recent years, the two major manufacturers--Hitachi and Fujitsu—have increasingly leased directly to customers as far as their cash flow permitted. The reason for this is the competitive nature of the market. Large users want a better price than is permitted by JECC's fixed price policy. If the large manufacturers do not try to accommodate these large users by dealing with them directly, the transaction would in all probability go to a foreign supplier.

When a new computer model appears, customers trade in the existing leased equipment, and the manufacturer must repurchase at JECC book value. As technology moved swiftly in the 1960s, the resale value of the equipment sank well below book value, which created a new financial problem for the manufacturers. MITI and the Ministry of Finance developed a tax reserve in which initially 10 percent, then 20 percent, of the original selling price to JECC could be reserved from taxable income against future estimated trade-in losses. After five years, the reserve had to be put back into the company's income stream. The cash flow effect of this provision reached a peak in 1972, when 10.3 billion yen in taxation was saved by the industry. Since then, budget pressure has forced a cutback in the provision. In 1977, 3 billion yen was saved.

To help clear the market of obsolete machines and make way for the new models, and to promote the use of computers among small businesses, the government has encouraged the Chambers of Commerce to repurchase traded-in leased machines from JECC. Resale price is set at 60 percent of the original book value; half is paid by government and one quarter each by the user and by the original manufacturer, who then charges it against his trade-in tax reserve. Total government subsidy in 1976 was 40 million yen.

Other devices to preserve the manufacturers' cash flow and develop the market have also been used. Special accelerated depreciation is extended to some computer production facilities. Special depreciation was also established in 1970 for the purchase of larger computers, which enabled buyers to write off 20 percent of initial book value in the first year in addition to normal depreciation. This provision aims to make the ownership of a computer more attractive than the leasing of foreign computers in Japan. Computers were also afforded preferential treatment in property taxation. Industry pays a standard local tax of 1.4 percent of taxable real assets every year; the taxable value of the computer can be reduced by 20 percent. There are miscellaneous other tax benefits, including a tax credit for training expenses for data processing engineers. The sums involved are far smaller than those committed to technology development and JECC.

Market Protection. The government has used both direct and indirect forms of market protection. Tariffs assessed against computers and semiconductors have always been high relative to Japan's other products. Quantitative restrictions on both components and computer systems were the last to be lifted in the mid-1970s. Until recently, MITI actively discouraged Japanese companies from buying foreign computers as long as a domestic offering met the specification. At present, however, the private sector computer market in Japan is essentially open. Western companies can import or manufacture what product they wish. Informal protection continues in the public sector market, which includes all of civilian government and military expenditure as well as a large portion of the university and research institute market. Consequently, while domestic producers have between 50 and 60 percent of the total Japanese market in value, they have over 90 percent of the public sector portion. The only exceptions to this informal rule arise when the Japanese supplier cannot meet the specifications or when a Japanese supplier subcontracts a key part of the system to a superior foreign supplier in order to outperform other domestic bidders. MITI does not like this practice, but it does occasionally happen.

In the semiconductor area, government purchases are confined to domestic producers, and, for different reasons, much of the private market is closed to foreign suppliers. Japanese computer and telecommunications equipment producers are both the major users and major suppliers of integrated circuits. Consequently, only where Western technology is unique or the cost is dramatically less are chips imported. The lengthy period of market protection posed a dilemma for MITI. The prohibition of any foreign investment into Japan, in either new ventures or existing domestic producers, preserved the industry's domestic character. As a consequence of this protection, producers were to some extent more dependent on MITI because of its influence on the market and the financial incentives it could provide. On the other hand, protection delayed any shakeout among the six producers, and there was not enough competitive pressure to make producers bend to MITI's consolidation schemes.

TELECOMMUNICATIONS

There are four major telecommunications equipment suppliers in Japan—Nippon Electric, Fujitsu, Oki, and Hitachi (the Big Four). MITI and the Ministry of Post and Telecommunications delegate most policy authority to Nippon Telephone and Telegraph Corporation (NTT), a public corporation charged with maintaining a domestic telecommunications network. The Ministry of Post and Telecommunications controls NTT and authorizes its budget; the directors of NTT are appointed by the Prime Minister with Diet approval. In addition to controlling the telephone and telegraph systems, NTT monopolizes all common carrier network transmission in Japan, including data, and offers data processing time-sharing services in competition with private companies. NTT also licenses all communications, including private microwave and citizen-band radios.

Japanese industrial policy in telecommunications has concentrated on supporting research and development and helping the industry to build an export capability by allowing high prices to be charged on domestic sales. Telecommunications research and development and system engineering is generally performed by NTT laboratories, much as Bell laboratories serves American Telephone and Telegraph Company in the United States. NTT makes all decisions on technical specifications, and engineers of the Big Four manufacturers are invited to develop new equipment jointly after basic research is completed by NTT's own engineers. Therefore all research and development expenses incurred by manufacturers are mostly application and production related. Since new equipment is jointly developed by NTT and its designated manufacturers, NTT assigns actual production and supply to each manufacturer, depending on availability of technical capacity and actual performance of the company on past assignments.

NTT's research and development program has evolved as competitive needs have changed. In the 1960s, development of each component was assigned to a manufacturer (e.g., the switch frame to Nippon Electric and high speed transmissions to Hitachi). In order to develop overall telecommunication/computer technology, however, all four manufacturers are now involved in jointly developing future technical specifications with NTT. Opportunities are given equally to manufacturers to learn everything, from the switching system components to materials technology.

In addition to assistance for research and development, NTT also helps its suppliers in financing exports. The relationship between NTT and its major suppliers—Fujitsu, Hitachi, and Oki—has helped these manufacturers to finance the growth of their businesses. First, prices are not bid but negotiated on a generous cost-plus basis (somewhat less generous in recent years because of NTT's operating losses). Profit margins are widely alleged to be higher on NTT business than on export sales, though figures are not publicly available. Second, the exclusion of foreign equipment stabilizes prices and production volumes. Third, NTT advances a portion of the purchase price to the manufacturer, in effect providing interest free funds. As a result of these factors, combined with NTT's financing of the research and development, the manufacturers can be very flexible in pricing exports. In this respect, Japanese producers enjoy an advantage over some major international competitors such as ITT and Ericsson.

Japanese companies got off to a late start in telecommunications exports, in large part because of their undistinguished technology. However, the boom in the OPEC and developing Asian markets in the middle and late 1970s, combined with lower growth at home, brought them into export markets. Exports—only 8 percent of sales in the early 1970s—are now 18-20 percent. Because of the higher investment required in the new generation of digital equipment, NTT is encouraging firms to export more in order to spread the revenue base. The indirect forms of assistance which have been indicated, combined with liberal financing from Japanese banks, have contributed significantly to this goal.

Telecommunications policy is closely related to that of computers, which brings the Ministry of Post and Telecommunications into close contact with MITI. Coordination of policy between them is difficult. MITI has pressed for a faster and more meaningful liberalization of imports in telecommunications equipment than MOPT has conceded. Disagreements arise over research directions and over data communications policy. The two ministries are being brought into more contact by the convergence of data processing and data communications technologies, and policy coordination will continue to be difficult.

SUMMARY

As with the nuclear reactor and aircraft industries, the computer and telecommunications industries have been the subject of government interest throughout the world. The U.S. Defense Department research and development funding and purchases were essential to the development of the miniature electronics industry in the United States, and governments have played a key role in the development of the computer and telecommunications industries in a number of European countries. Japan continues to make a large commitment to information electronics. It is too early to tell whether these policies will be successful. The Japanese still have not achieved technological parity, and the strong, aggressive U.S. leaders are unlikely to follow the mistakes of their counterparts in steel and consumer electronics.

POSTSCRIPT

In this booklet we have focused on two distinguishing facets of Japanese industrial policy: the economic and competitive principles that underlie it and the broad-based, interactive process through which policy is generated. Together they help to produce good, workable policy and provide a clear framework within which businesses can develop their strategies.

It is important to keep these two strengths in mind as we look to the future. Commentators who attribute Japan's success to date principally to a labor price advantage, unfair trade practices, and government protection of domestic markets typically argue that Japan's trade performance will level off now that Japan is no longer trying to catch up with the West. Japanese industrial wages are now equal to the European average, competitor countries are strictly enforcing their laws against unfair export practices, and Japan's markets have essentially been opened.

Since we do not credit these factors as essential to Japan's success historically, we do not believe their absence will be critical in the future. Instead we look to the transition that Japan is making in its industrial structure and policies. Japan no longer tries to compete seriously in businesses where wage rates are central to a competitive cost position. Japan's modern manufacturing companies remain profitable, continue to invest, and are probably more confident than at any time before. Government policy toward industry remains very active, though its targets have changed. It has shifted focus from protecting markets and bringing Japan's production scale up to Western standards toward selectively placing major research and development funds, financing important plant export deals, and restructuring declining industries. In short, Japan's momentum and the thoughtfulness and determination behind its new directions should not be underestimated.

This is not to say, however, that Japan will continue to succeed competitively. Rather it is to say that if Japan's impact on world markets withers, the cause will not be changes that have taken place internally within Japan, but changes in the behavior of its competitors—both companies and countries. Serious Western executives and industrial policymakers are increasingly coming to understand the corporate and national policies and behavior which have attended the surrender in certain areas of their international business and economic leadership. The more alert of them are responding with longer and more realistic planning-time horizons, greater investment in the critical competitive areas, and more broad-based policy discussions among the constituencies affected by industrial policy, including governments, management, labor, and banks, to promote consensus.

For many government and business organizations where the traditional culture resists this view, this change may be difficult. But it is becoming increasingly clear that in a sophisticated international competitive world, traditional government policy focusing on macroeconomic variables alone is no longer adequate. Similarly, corporations cannot continue to rely on those strategies which brought them leadership in the domestic market. Finally, government, business, labor, and finance can no longer establish policy separately. As Western companies and governments learn these lessons, the competitive environment faced by the Japanese will toughen.

There is of course a great danger in transposing the experiences of one society on another. We have been generally positive about Japanese industrial performance by both government and industry, though we have pointed out many mistakes and failures. While the basic economic and competitive principles of Japan's approach should be instructive, neither its manner of making and carrying out policy nor the specific themes and programs of Japanese industrial policy need be appropriate to any other nation. The lessons for Western economies are more subtle than direct. They have more to do with the discipline of analysis and the importance of consensus than with the elaborateness of specific plans or the spending of large sums of money.

IRA C. MAGAZINER is a founding partner of Telesis, a consulting company specializing in long-term economic and industrial policy for governments and international strategy for corporations. He worked for six years with the Boston Consulting Group, during which time he managed cases in a variety of industries for Western and Japanese clients. He was educated at Brown University and spent two years as a Rhodes Scholar at Balliol College, Oxford.

THOMAS M. HOUT is a vice-president of the Boston Consulting Group. He holds a Bachelor's degree in Economics from Yale University, a Master's degree in Business Administration from Stanford University, and he attended Manchester University. He has lived in Japan, and has consulted on the Japanese business system for corporations and governments. He is co-author (with James C. Abegglen) of *Japan in 1980* (London, 1974) and "Facing Up to the Trade Gap with Japan," *Foreign Affairs*, Autumn 1978, as well as a contributor to *Japan: The Government-Business Relationship* (U.S. Department of Commerce, 1972).

INSTITUTE OF INTERNATIONAL STUDIES
UNIVERSITY OF CALIFORNIA, BERKELEY

CARL G. ROSBERG,
Director

Monographs published by the Institute include:

RESEARCH SERIES

1. *The Chinese Anarchist Movement*, by Robert A. Scalapino and George T. Yu. ($1.00)
7. *Birth Rates in Latin America: New Estimates of Historical Trends*, by O. Andrew Collver. ($2.50)
15. *Central American Economic Integration: The Politics of Unequal Benefits*, by Stuart I. Fagan. ($2.00)
16. *The International Imperatives of Technology: Technological Development and the International Political System*, by Eugene B. Skolnikoff. ($2.95)
17. *Autonomy or Dependence as Regional Integration Outcomes: Central America*, by Philippe C. Schmitter. ($1.75)
19. *Entry of New Competitors in Yugoslav Market Socialism*, by S.R. Sacks. ($2.50)
20. *Political Integration in French-Speaking Africa*, by Abdul A. Jalloh. ($3.50)
21. *The Desert and the Sown: Nomads in the Wider Society*, ed. by Cynthia Nelson. ($5.50)
22. *U.S.-Japanese Competition in International Markets: A Study of the Trade-Investment Cycle in Modern Capitalism*, by John E. Roemer. ($3.95)
23. *Political Disaffection Among British University Students: Concepts, Measurement, and Causes*, by Jack Citrin and David J. Elkins. ($2.00)
24. *Urban Inequality and Housing Policy in Tanzania: The Problem of Squatting*, by Richard E. Stren. ($2.95)
25. *The Obsolescence of Regional Integration Theory*, by Ernst B. Haas. ($4.95)
26. *The Voluntary Service Agency in Israel*, by Ralph M. Kramer. ($2.00)
27. *The SOCSIM Demographic-Sociological Microsimulation Program: Operating Manual*, by Eugene A. Hammel et al. ($4.50)
28. *Authoritarian Politics in Communist Europe: Uniformity & Diversity in One-Party States*, ed. by Andrew C. Janos. ($3.95)
29. *The Anglo-Icelandic Cod War of 1972-1973: A Case Study of a Fishery Dispute*, by Jeffrey A. Hart. ($2.00)
30. *Plural Societies and New States: A Conceptual Analysis*, by Robert Jackson ($2.00)
31. *The Politics of Crude Oil Pricing in the Middle East, 1970-1975: A Study in International Bargaining*, by Richard Chadbourn Weisberg. ($4.95)
32. *Agricultural Policy and Performance in Zambia: History, Prospects, and Proposals for Change*, by Doris Jansen Dodge. ($4.95)
33. *Five Classy Programs: Computer Procedures for the Classification of Households*, by E.A. Hammel and R.Z. Deuel. ($3.75)
34. *Housing the Urban Poor in Africa: Policy, Politics, and Bureaucracy in Mombasa*, by Richard E. Stren. ($5.95)
35. *The Russian New Right: Right-Wing Ideologies in the Contemporary USSR*, by Alexander Yanov. ($5.95)
36. *Social Change in Romania, 1860-1940: A Debate on Development in a European Nation*, ed. by Kenneth Jowitt. ($4.50)
37. *The Leninist Response to National Dependency*, by Kenneth Jowitt. ($3.25)
38. *Socialism in Sub-Saharan Africa: A New Assessment*, ed. by Carl G. Rosberg and Thomas M. Callaghy. ($12.95)
39. *Tanzania's Ujamaa Villages: The Implementation of a Rural Development Strategy*, by Dean E. McHenry, Jr. ($5.95)
40. *Who Gains from Deep Ocean Mining: Simulating the Impact of Regimes for Regulating Nodule Exploitation*, by I.G. Bulkley. ($3.50)

INSTITUTE OF INTERNATIONAL STUDIES MONOGRAPHS (continued)

41. *Industrialization, Industrialists, and the Nation-State in Peru: A Comparative/Sociological Analysis*, by Frits Wils. ($5.95)
42. *Ideology, Public Opinion, and Welfare Policy: Attitudes toward Taxes and Spending in Industrialized Societies*, by Richard M. Coughlin. ($6.50)
43. *The Apartheid Regime: Political Power and Racial Domination*, ed. by Robert M. Price and Carl G. Rosberg. ($12.50)
44. *The Yugoslav Economic System and Its Performance in the 1970s*, by Laura D'Andrea Tyson. ($4.95)
45. *Conflict in Chad*, by Virginia Thompson and Richard Adloff. ($7.50)
46. *Conflict and Coexistence in Belgium: The Dynamics of a Culturally Divided Society*, ed. by Arend Lijphart. ($7.50)

POLITICS OF MODERNIZATION SERIES

1. *Spanish Bureaucratic-Patrimonialism in America*, by Magali Sarfatti. ($2.00)
2. *Civil-Military Relations in Argentina, Chile, and Peru*, by Liisa North. ($2.00)
3. *Notes on the Process of Industrialization in Argentina, Chile, and Peru*, by Alcira Leiserson. ($1.75)
9. *Modernization and Bureaucratic-Authoritarianism: Studies in South American Politics*, by Guillermo O'Donnell. ($7.95)

POLICY PAPERS IN INTERNATIONAL AFFAIRS

1. *Images of Detente and the Soviet Political Order*, by Kenneth Jowitt. ($1.25)
2. *Detente After Brezhnev: The Domestic Roots of Soviet Foreign Policy*, by Alexander Yanov. ($4.50)
3. *The Mature Neighbor Policy: A New United States Economic Policy for Latin America*, by Albert Fishlow. ($3.95)
4. *Five Images of the Soviet Future: A Critical Review and Synthesis*, by G.W. Breslauer. ($4.50)
5. *Global Evangelism Rides Again: How to Protect Human Rights Without Really Trying*, by Ernst B. Haas. ($2.95)
6. *Israel and Jordan: Implications of an Adversarial Partnership*, by Ian Lustick ($2.00)
7. *Political Syncretism in Italy: Historical Coalition Strategies and the Present Crisis*, by Giuseppe Di Palma. ($3.95)
8. *U.S. Foreign Policy in Sub-Saharan Africa: National Interest and Global Strategy*, by Robert M. Price. ($2.25)
9. *East-West Technology Transfer in Perspective*, by R.J. Carrick. ($2.75)
10. *NATO's Unremarked Demise*, by Earl C. Ravenal. ($2.00)
11. *Toward an Africanized U.S. Policy for Southern Africa: A Strategy for Increasing Political Leverage*, by Ronald T. Libby. ($5.50)
12. *The Taiwan Relations Act and the Defense of the Republic of China*, by Edwin K. Snyder et al. ($3.95)
13. *Cuba's Policy in Africa, 1959-1980*, by William M. LeoGrande. ($4.50)
14. *Norway, NATO, and the Forgotten Soviet Challenge*, by Kirsten Amundsen. ($2.95)
15. *Japanese Industrial Policy*, by Ira C. Magaziner and Thomas M. Hout. ($6.50)
16. *Containment, Soviet Behavior, and Grand Strategy*, by Robert E. Osgood. ($5.50)
17. *U.S.-Japanese Competition in the Semiconductor Industry: A Study in International Trade and Technological Development*, by M. Borrus, J. Millstein, and J. Zysman ($7.50)

Address correspondence to:

Institute of International Studies
215 Moses Hall
University of California
Berkeley, California 94720

d